How to Engage, Involve, and Motivate Employees

Also by Janis Allen

Performance Teams: Creating the Feedback Loop

I Saw What You Did & I Know Who You Are: Bloopers, Blunders, and Success Stories on Giving and Receiving Recognition

Team Up!

You Made My Day: Creating Co-Worker Recognition & Relationships (with Michael McCarthy)

Stories from a Sandy Mush Girl (memoir)

Also by Michael McCarthy

You Made My Day: Creating Co-Worker Recognition & Relationships (with Janis Allen)

Sustain Your Gains: The People Side of Lean-Six Sigma

The Noah Option (political thriller)

The Rainbow Option (political thriller)

How to Engage, Involve, and Motivate Employees

Building a Culture of Lean Leadership with Two-Way Commitment and Communication

By

Janis Allen

Michael McCarthy

CRC Press
Taylor & Francis Group

CRC Press is an imprint of the
Taylor & Francis Group, an **informa** business
A PRODUCTIVITY PRESS BOOK

CRC Press
Taylor & Francis Group
6000 Broken Sound Parkway NW, Suite 300
Boca Raton, FL 33487-2742

Printed on acid-free paper

International Standard Book Number-13: 978-1-4987-7775-9 (Paperback)

Library of Congress Cataloging-in-Publication Data

Names: Allen, Janis, 1950- author.
Title: How to engage, involve, and motivate employees : building a culture of lean leadership with two-way commitment and communication / Janis Allen.
Description: Boca Raton : CRC Press, 2017. | Includes index.
Identifiers: LCCN 2016038702| ISBN 9781498777759 (pbk. : alk. paper) | ISBN 9781315154954 (eBook)
Subjects: LCSH: Employee motivation. | Achievement motivation. | Interpersonal relations. | Trust. | Leadership.
Classification: LCC HF5549.5.M63 A528 2017 | DDC 658.3/14--dc23
LC record available at https://lccn.loc.gov/2016038702

Visit the Taylor & Francis Web site at
http://www.taylorandfrancis.com

and the CRC Press Web site at
http://www.crcpress.com

Printed and bound in the United States of America by Sheridan

Dedicated to Dr. Aubrey C. Daniels
You taught us, inspired us, trusted us, and befriended us.

Janis and Mike
July 2016

All improvement takes place project by project...
– Dr. Joseph M. Juran
Quality Control Handbook

The key leader behavior to start engagement is asking questions.
– Michael McCarthy, author of
Sustain Your Gains: The People Side of Lean-Six Sigma

The way to sustain any behavior is with positive reinforcement.
– Dr. Aubrey C. Daniels, author of
Bringing Out the Best in People

Notice good work ... and make your notice noticed.
– Janis Allen, coauthor of
You Made My Day: Creating Co-Worker Recognition & Relationships

Get a team you trust and then trust your team.
– Michel J. Robertson
President, Accountability Business Systems

Contents

Foreword xiii

Engage, Involve, and Motivate Employees: 5-Step Method xv

Authors xvii

1 What Is Engagement? **1**

What Engagement IS NOT 2

What Engagement IS 5

First, Do No Harm 7

Summary Checklist 10

2 Why Engage, Involve, and Motivate Employees? **11**

Select Measurable Goals That Benefit Your Organization and Your Customers 11

Engage and Involve People to Improve the Processes to Meet These Goals 14

Summary Checklist 16

3 5-Step Method to Engage, Involve, and Motivate Employees **17**

4 Find Projects to PULL People **21**

A. Find an Improvement Project. It Will *PULL People* and Their Knowledge, Experience, Skills, and Interest 21

B. What Projects? Look at Your Organization's Quality and Delivery Goals and Your Customers' Needs 22

C. How? Go to the Workplace and Look for Things to Improve. Ask Your Employees What They SEE That Needs Improvement (These Are Potential Projects) 28

What's the Difference between PUSH and PULL? 31

Summary Checklist 34

5 Ask for Ideas on Specific Improvements 35

A. Ask for Help on a Specific Project or Problem 36

For Team Involvement 41

B. Accept Ideas Gratefully and Acknowledge Them (Even before Determining if the Ideas Can Be Used) 41

C. Pick One to Three Ideas to Test. Remember, Your Action Here Is to *Select*, Not to Judge, Criticize, or Eliminate Ideas 42

Picking Ideas to Test 42

D. Level the Ideas So Decisions Can Be Made and/or Actions Can Be Taken Immediately 43

Summary Checklist 46

6 Set Time Targets to Test Ideas and Complete Action Steps 47

A. Set Time Targets for Testing Ideas and Completing Action Steps 48

B. Coach Individuals to Help Them Perform Their Project Action Steps... 48

C. Recognize People for Completing Their Action Steps on the Project.... 50

Summary Checklist 58

7 Motivate Actions with Positive Recognition 59

A. Give People a Positive Reason to Get Engaged 60

B. Recognition Is an Action That Shows Respect for Another Person's Effort or Achievement. Recognition Motivates Ideas and Actions 61

C. Four Ways to Make Your Recognition Effective and Prevent Unintended Blunders 63

1. When You Give Recognition, Be Very Specific about What You're Recognizing 63
2. Let Your Recognition Stand Alone 66
3. Personalize Your Recognition in Two Ways 67
4. Give Positive Recognition for Specific *Earned* Actions, Not Just to Be Nice 68

D. People Remember Your Words and Actions to Figure Out What's Acceptable and What's Unacceptable; This Creates Your Culture 69

Summary Checklist 72

8 Coach with Feedback: Verbal, Data, and Graphs 73

A. Tell and Show People Frequently (Daily or Twice a Week) How They Are Making Progress on the Project, and What They Can Do to Improve 74

B. Coach Employees to Use Graphs and Checklists to Track Project Progress 75

For Team Feedback 76

C. Check Your Progress on Results (% On-Time Delivery, etc.) from the Date You Made the Process/Project Change.....77
Summary Checklist.....78

9 Complete, Then Repeat.....79

10 How Many People to Engage? Let the Project PULL the Number of People.....81
A. Start with Your Project, Problem, or Needed Improvement.....82
B. Determine the Type of General Skills and Specific "How-to" Knowledge You'll Need to Work Your Project.....82
C. Recruit Individual(s) Who Have the General Skills and the Specific "How-to" Knowledge.....83
D. Engage the Individual(s) by Asking for Their Help. Build a Team if Needed, One Person at a Time. Use Projects to PULL People.....83
E. Aim for Four to Six People on Your Team.....87
Summary Checklist.....88

11 How Project Teams Create Motivation.....89
A. People Are Motivated by Having Their Opinions Valued.....89
B. People Are Motivated by Being "In on Things".....89
C. People Are Motivated by Feeling Part of a Team.....90
Projects Pull Pride.....91
Summary Checklist.....92

12 Build a Culture of Trust with Your Actions.....93
Definitions.....93
A. Your Actions as a Leader Can Be Trust-builders or Trust-busters.....94
B. Tell the Truth, Even if It's Difficult for Both People in the Conversation.....94
C. Do What You Say You Will Do.....96
D. Never Make Negative Statements about Other Employees. Tell Them to Their Faces What You Want Them to Improve.....98
E. Give Credit Where It's Earned.....100
Summary Checklist.....102

13 How to Measure Your Success.....103
A. Measure: Individuals Doing Things.....104
B. Measure: Teams Explaining Their Projects.....104
C. Measure Your Role: Leader Standard Work to Engage, Involve, and Motivate.....107
Summary Checklist.....108

14 When Correcting Is Needed: Deal with Negatives and Move On 109

A. Deal with Negative Issues Individually (Not in Groups), Specifically (No Generalities), and Quickly (No Procrastinating). Then, Move On 110

B. Coach for Correct Behaviors and Give Recognition When the Person Improves 111

Correcting with the Help of a Checklist 113

Summary Checklist 116

15 FMMs (Frequently Made Mistakes): Troubleshooting and Preventing Them 117

A. Don't Start an "Engagement Program" for Scores on a Survey. Don't Start an "Engagement Program" if You Aren't Prepared to Follow Up on the Employee Ideas You Receive 118

B. Deal with Negative Talk and Behaviors by Choosing Where Your Attention Goes. Give No Attention to Negative Talk. Give Your Attention to Productive Talk 120

C. Learn from Past Mistakes 122

Increasing Successes 123

Summary Checklist 124

16 Grow More Leaders 125

How Someone Grew Me as a Leader 125

Summary Checklist 128

Appendix I 129

Appendix II 131

Appendix III 133

Appendix IV 135

Appendix V 139

Appendix VI 141

Appendix VII 145

Glossary 155

Resources 159

Index 163

Foreword

Employee engagement and having an idea-generating culture are often the missing links to sustainable, long-term growth for any company.

Unfortunately, most companies miss the mark by a long shot. They chase the wrong metrics, overemphasize employee surveys, and don't truly, empathetically listen to their workforce.

As any manager or CEO will tell you, it's challenging for sure. They're unsure how to create a structure to capture employee ideas, reward them appropriately, and make this commonplace rather than the exception.

Thankfully, performance/process improvement experts Mike McCarthy and Janis Allen have solved this for all of us with their new book. It's packed with real-life examples of the dos and don'ts of driving employee engagement throughout your operation. Whether you're the CEO, a front-line supervisor, or a team leader, their structured, step-by-step approach will remove all the guesswork from this challenging process.

Devour this book, follow their lessons, take action, and watch as a culture of engagement takes hold. Your operation will never be the same again.

David Visco, 5S Expert
Founder and President, The 5S Store
President, AME Northeast Region
Author, 5S Made Easy

Engage, Involve, and Motivate Employees: 5-Step Method

1. Find Projects to PULL People
2. Ask for Ideas on Specific Improvements
3. Set Time Targets to Test Ideas and Complete Action Steps
4. Motivate Actions with Positive Recognition
5. Coach with Feedback: Verbal, Data, and Graphs

Authors

Janis Allen has been an HR manager for a major textile manufacturer, a performance consultant, and vice president of operations for Aubrey Daniels International. She has owned Performance Leadership Consulting since 1991. She created the book *Performance Teams*, training materials, and the implementation processes that combined Quality Circles with Performance Management for Xerox Refurbishing and Xerox Distribution. Some of her clients include BMW Manufacturing, 3M, Philadelphia Electric, Blue Cross and Blue Shield, Wisconsin Gas, International Paper, and the New York Department of Motor Vehicles. Janis was a keynote speaker for the National Association for Employee Recognition. Her earlier book on recognition, *I Saw What You Did and I Know Who You Are*, was used by Delta Airlines. She and her husband and coauthor Michael McCarthy wrote *You Made My Day: Creating Co-Worker Recognition & Relationships*. They live in the Blue Ridge Mountains of North Carolina.

Michael McCarthy has worked with work teams, supervisors, and top executives as a process/performance improvement consultant, Lean trainer/coach, and curriculum designer. He was Executive Director for Corporate and Economic Development at Asheville-Buncombe Technical College in Asheville, North Carolina, and a manager in Accenture's Change Management Practice. As senior consultant with Aubrey Daniels International, some of his clients were Preston Trucking (a case study in the book *A Great Place to Work*),

3M, Georgia Power, Department of the Army, Ford Motor Credit, Emerson Electronics and Space Division, Fireman's Fund Insurance, and Black & Decker. Based on his book *Sustain Your Gains: The People Side of Lean-Six Sigma*, Mike was a keynote speaker for the 2015 European Behavior-Based Safety Conference in Bologna, Italy.

Chapter 1

What Is Engagement?

Engagement is action, not survey scores.

Key Points

A. What engagement IS NOT
B. What engagement IS

Definitions

Engage: *To gain and hold attention and interest; to ask to participate*
Involve: *To help people take actions*
Motivate: *To inspire a person to* **want** *to do something*

At a manufacturing plant for cathode-ray tubes, moisture was found inside some of the tubes, causing quality problems. Supervisors tried unsuccessfully to find the cause of the moisture. Engineers couldn't figure it out.

When a supervisor mentioned it to one of his machine operators, the operator said, "I know what's causing it. Every once in a while, I notice an excess of moisture in the CO2 line, and I purge it to get rid of the moisture."

The supervisor asked, "Why didn't you say something?"

The operator replied, "No one ever asked me." (This story is from Dr. Aubrey Daniels, author of *Bringing Out the Best in People*.)

Contrast that story with this one. On a snowy day at Preston Trucking (one of Mike's clients), a driver was unable to make his scheduled deliveries in his truck. He went home, put chains on the tires of his personal pickup truck, came to the terminal, loaded the freight into his pickup, and delivered it on schedule.

Which of these stories would describe your current work culture? Of course, we all want the initiative, engagement, involvement, and motivation of the truck driver. This book will show you how to get it.

You've heard the old saying "two heads are better than one." Multiply "one" by the number of employees in your organization. That indicates the extra experience, energy, and ideas you have the potential to tap. That's engagement and involvement.

Would you like employees to mechanically follow your instructions and processes, doing just enough to get by? Or would you prefer that they *engage* (apply their attention, experience, energy, and brainpower) and become *involved* (take actions) to make the improvements that will help your organization grow and add jobs?

Unless your employees are very different from those we've met in more than three decades of working in health care, manufacturing, and service businesses, we can promise you four things:

1. Most employees have more and better ideas than you might imagine.
2. Most are more willing to become involved than you might expect.
3. Most will enjoy learning new skills and finding ways to improve the work.
4. Most will voluntarily offer extra effort if they receive acknowledgment (recognition) for their ideas.

You can test for yourself whether these four things are true. If you use the easy tools in this book, we're confident you will build an engaged and motivated workforce. If you already have engagement and involvement, you can take it to the next level with these ideas.

What Engagement IS NOT

- Engagement survey scores
- Number of kaizen events
- Number of teams

- Number of team meetings
- Merely satisfying the "check-the-box" requirements of corporate, a union, or a customer/supplier agreement

Janis's example

A refurbishing company had decided to implement quality teams after its union asked for more employee involvement. At the end of a year, one facility had 12 teams operating. When asked what the results were, the answer was, "We have 12 involvement teams. That satisfies our agreement with the union."

On attending some of the team meetings, I found these projects being discussed:

1. *Where to move the watercooler*
2. *Who should clean the microwave in the break room*

Many of the members of these teams weren't happy to attend the team meetings. Some said they considered them a waste of time and would rather be on the job working. On top of that, their coworkers criticized them for "sitting in the training room doing nothing," because no one (inside or outside the teams) could see any tangible results of their meetings.

What went wrong? Unfortunately, this organization had chosen the wrong goal: teams for the sake of teams, involvement for the sake of involvement. The monthly reports they sent to their division management stated simply the number of active teams. There was no reporting of how productivity problems were solved or how work processes were improved.

Before you read the rest of the story, list your ideas for actions that you think could have prevented the unfortunate experience described in the story:

	Better Ways to Begin Our Engagement/Involvement Efforts
1.	
2.	
3.	

Now, to continue the story

To rescue these teams, I included their team leaders in the groups, and gave them measurable performance goals, such as efficiency, delivery, quality, waste reduction, and customer service. I trained them to use data, feedback, goals, and recognition. When they began working on these meaty issues, not only did they make measurable contributions to the organization, but their peers began to **respect their work**, *and—surprise—managers found it easy to give the teams positive recognition for their work (where before managers and supervisors had resented their time away from the job).*

Engagement is not just for the sake of engagement, so we can say, "We have an engagement program," or "We held 10 kaizen events this year," or "Our engagement survey scores are high."

So first, **identify the purpose** of employee engagement and involvement, aligned with your organization's goals.* Ask your teams to work on those **specific goals** and **train them to use data** and **set goals**. **Coach** them and **give positive recognition** for productive behaviors and results. Focus on measurable results. Everyone will win.

Setting Up Engagement Teams	
 **Wrong Way**	"Corporate says we have to have teams. Pick some people and tell them they can go to the training room and brainstorm for 30 minutes a week."
 **Right Way**	"We need to reduce the defects on product X. Customers are complaining about it. Let's ask an employee whose experience will help us reduce defects. Show her or him how to use data to analyze problem causes and identify potential solutions. We can add team members as needed."

* Goals should be tied to this question: Do they end up getting the product or service in the hands of the customers faster, more easily, cheaper, or with higher quality?

What Engagement IS

If an outsider comes into your organization and asks, "Are your employees engaged?" you could say, "Sure they are. Let me show you the results of our last engagement survey." If this is your only focus, you're confusing the by-product with the actual product. If someone asked you, "Is your carpenter a skilled craftsman?" you wouldn't say, "Sure he is. Let me show you his tools." Don't confuse the tool with the action. Watch the craftsman at work to observe his skills and look at the product of his work.

So, when the outsider comes into your workplace and asks, "Are your employees engaged?" say, "Let's go talk to them. Then you decide." Take that outsider to the work area and introduce him to an employee. Say, "Allie, would you show our visitor your charts outlining your latest team project and show him the changes the team made on the shop floor?" If your employees can do this, they are actively engaged.

Everyone says employee engagement and involvement are key to the success of the organization. There are many engagement surveys designed to learn how engaged employees feel about their employers. In this book, you'll learn how to engage the brains and improvement *actions* of all employees, not just change their answers on a survey.

> The purpose of employee engagement is to make improvements people can be proud of.

Why isn't it enough to measure engagement by survey numbers? Imagine you are a manager of nursing. You have just bought all new instruments for your nursing staff. Your goal is to improve the accuracy of patient data (on their vital signs taken) and improve the consistency of daily recordings. To get a return on your investment, you want to know if your nurses are engaged, involved, and motivated to use the new instruments. You ask your nursing supervisor to complete an inventory survey and she does.

- New thermometers: check
- New blood pressure cuffs: check
- New stethoscopes: check
- All instruments: check
- At the end of the month, you notice that patient data are not being recorded completely and on time. You go to the department and find that the new instruments are still in their packages.

This is a common mistake: confusing "survey data" with action. What you want, of course, is action and improvement. A survey is only a tool. It's not activity (usage). It is not engagement.

When your focus is on a measurement tool rather than the actions you want, you get off track. If you only looked at the speedometer while driving, you'd run off the road!

Many employees don't tell the truth on engagement surveys; they say what they think management expects them to say. And in case this so-called anonymous survey isn't really anonymous, who wants to be the one who says, "I'm not engaged"? This is another reason survey data are not an accurate indicator of *actual engagement*.

At an airline departure gate, we heard the announcement, "Please complete our customer survey when you receive the e-mail. We want you to rate us a five, not a four. Five is alive; four is out the door. Ha ha. Just to help you remember to rate us a five, we have this basket of snacks here on the counter for you. Help yourselves. It's not a bribe or anything."

Beware of surveys. People have all kinds of wrong motives for the ratings they give on surveys.

Engagement isn't checked boxes on a survey.

It's improvement actions in the workplace.

Engagement is not limited to teams or groups. Individuals can engage in many ways: formal kaizen events, longer-term project teams, daily kaizen time, and day-to-day individual initiatives.

As a leader, you can show people how *they* can take actions to make improvements *they* can be proud of. You can help them to do it. Then, a good side effect is that their answers on engagement surveys will improve. The survey improvement will be based on making solutions work, their good results, and the satisfying feeling of being on a team. Then, your survey results will be based on *actions* and *their real experience*, not just words!

Pinch Point Warning #1: Don't make the mistake of focusing only on survey results. Even the most uninvolved employee can check the "I'm engaged" box on a survey. Instead, ask people for ideas on improvements *they* can make. Then, recruit a team to test the idea.

A survey is only a tool. It's not engagement.

First, Do No Harm

At one of Janis's client's, management announced a new program welcoming suggestions from employees. A machine operator went to his supervisor to suggest a way to improve the work process on his line. The supervisor said, "I don't pay you to think; I pay you to work. So, tomorrow morning when you come in, just leave that big brain of yours in your car."

The operator answered, "I can't sir. I drive a compact car." *He never offered another idea to the supervisor*. His motivation was turned off.

Does this story make you want to stand up and cheer for the operator? You can see the disconnect between what the managers *said they wanted* and the actual *response* by the supervisor.

We'll show you the correct response in Step 2 of the 5-Step Method. With the best of intentions, leaders have tried to use "programs" to increase employee engagement, but with limited or even detrimental results. For the supervisor who shut down the employee's suggestion, we suggest "The Engagement Hippocratic Oath." (It's just like the oath for physicians.)

First, do no harm.

Do no harm to your employees' motivation and trust.

In this book, you'll learn what works and what doesn't work. You and your employees will learn to use the tools, and then expand your skills of engagement, involvement, and motivation to include more and more employees in your organization.

You'll learn the benefits of

- Specific communication (what needs improving?)
- Asking rather than telling
- Listening rather than talking
- Motivating with positive recognition
- Setting goals, coaching, and helping each other complete projects

Engaging, involving, and motivating employees is not a company program. It's what *you* do. You, as an individual leader, on a daily basis. You are the engager. You are the involver. You are the motivator. You are the coach of your team.

These positive actions are easy and don't cost a nickel. You just need to make them a habit, part of your "Lean Leader Standard Work."

The great news is that each positive action radiates out from you like ripples in a pond, spreading your good efforts. So let's get started!

Engagement IS employees making improvements.
Engagement IS NOT survey scores or number of kaizen events.

QUIZ (answers on next page)	
1.	What engagement is: ______________________________
2.	What engagement is not: ____________________________

ANSWERS TO QUIZ	
1.	Engagement IS employees making improvements.
2.	Engagement IS NOT survey scores or number of kaizen events.

Summary Checklist

- Make sure you're not focusing your efforts on surveys, # of teams, # of kaizen events, or other measures that engagement IS NOT.
- Focus on improvement projects and people's actions—that's what engagement IS.

Chapter 2

Why Engage, Involve, and Motivate Employees?

Key Points

A. Select measurable goals that benefit your organization and your customers.
B. Engage and involve people to improve the processes to meet these goals.

Working to engage, involve, and motivate employees takes time and effort. Why do it?

- For better results
- For easier ways to keep the process flowing and get the work done … that's why!

Select Measurable Goals That Benefit Your Organization and Your Customers

Here are examples of three organizations' successes:

1. **Insurance Company: Increased Quantity of Work While Maintaining Quality**
   An insurance company tripled its number of claims processed per day while keeping quality high.

Here's how they did it:

Section leaders

Average Claims Processed per Team Member per Day

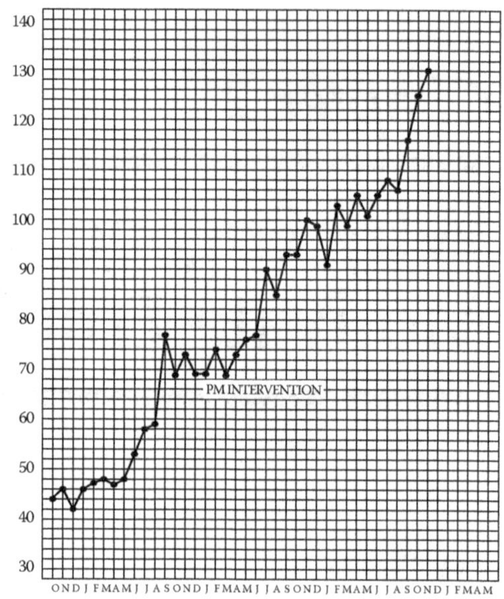

- Posted graphs daily for each team showing the average number of claims processed per employee per day (no individual names were posted).
- Asked employees for their ideas on how to process more claims without increasing errors. Some of the employees' ideas were
  - To modify the work flow to reduce seasonal backlogs
  - That each employee would begin tallying and reporting his or her own number of claims processed daily
- Gave private weekly feedback to individuals on their number of claims processed, and their quality.
- Gave specific positive recognition to employees for both their ideas and for their individual improvements.

The morale of the section teams rose because they were proud of their achievements shown on their graphs. Settling a claim faster, of course, made the customers happier. Happier customers will recommend the company to their friends. A virtuous circle!

2. **Transportation Company: Reduced Costs**

In a two-year period, a trucking company saved $2.4 million in fuel costs and $100,000 in labor costs for rebuilding engines. How? Here's what the supervisors and teams did:

- Posted graphs showing fuel costs and engine rebuild time
- Asked employees to brainstorm for improvement ideas
- Coached employees on behaviors to improve these areas
- Gave individual positive recognition for ideas and results
- Told the stories about individuals' and teams' successes to other people within the organization
- Invited employees to explain their improvements to senior managers and to visiting customers

> When customers from Rubbermaid visited this company's terminal, one of the managers spotted a pallet of Rubbermaid products on a lift truck and said to the driver, "Be careful with those, please. I work for Rubbermaid." Quick as a wink, the driver replied, "I do, too, sir!"

The driver demonstrated that he knew that the customer (indirectly) paid his salary. The Rubbermaid manager went back to headquarters and told senior leaders, "We have to do more business with these people!"

3. **Engineering Company: On-Time Delivery, Improved Quality, and Reduced Costs**

An engineering company designed equipment for military aircraft. For a radar indicator for the US Navy, the project team cut costs by 75% compared with previous projects, delivered the product early, and proved that it performed with three times the reliability of previous products manufactured by that facility. How did they do it?

- At the beginning of the project, a team was formed including both design engineers and production engineers, along with their supervisors. Their goal was to avoid past problems, such as presenting the design engineers' "finished" design to the production engineers, who then came back to them and said, "We can't make this work. You'll have to change the design."
- Team members created ways to track their work and communicate during the design process that prevented errors during production and testing.
- The team tracked its own expenses weekly to stay within its weekly budget, including its own labor costs, as well as materials costs.
- To ensure on-time delivery, the team graphed its percentage of actions completed on time, posted the graph in the work area, and reviewed each action during its weekly team meetings.
- Team members gave positive recognition to each other privately and at team meetings for their action items completed and for the weekly data showing their budget performance.

Engage and Involve People to Improve the Processes to Meet These Goals

Using the 5-Step Method in this book, you can get results like those described in the examples you just read. Here is a preview of Step 1:

The Purpose of Engaging and Involving Employees	
 **Wrong Way**	"Everybody's talking about employee engagement. Let's do it and see if it will make our employees happier."
 **Right Way**	"I suspect our employees have some great ideas about improving delivery to customers without sacrificing quality. Let's ask them to work on improving our on-time delivery."

QUIZ (answer on next page)	
1.	Select measurable _________ that benefit your organization and your customers.

ANSWER TO QUIZ	
1.	goals

Summary Checklist

- Select measurable goals that benefit your organization and your customers.
- Engage and involve people to improve the processes to meet these goals.

Chapter 3

5-Step Method to Engage, Involve, and Motivate Employees

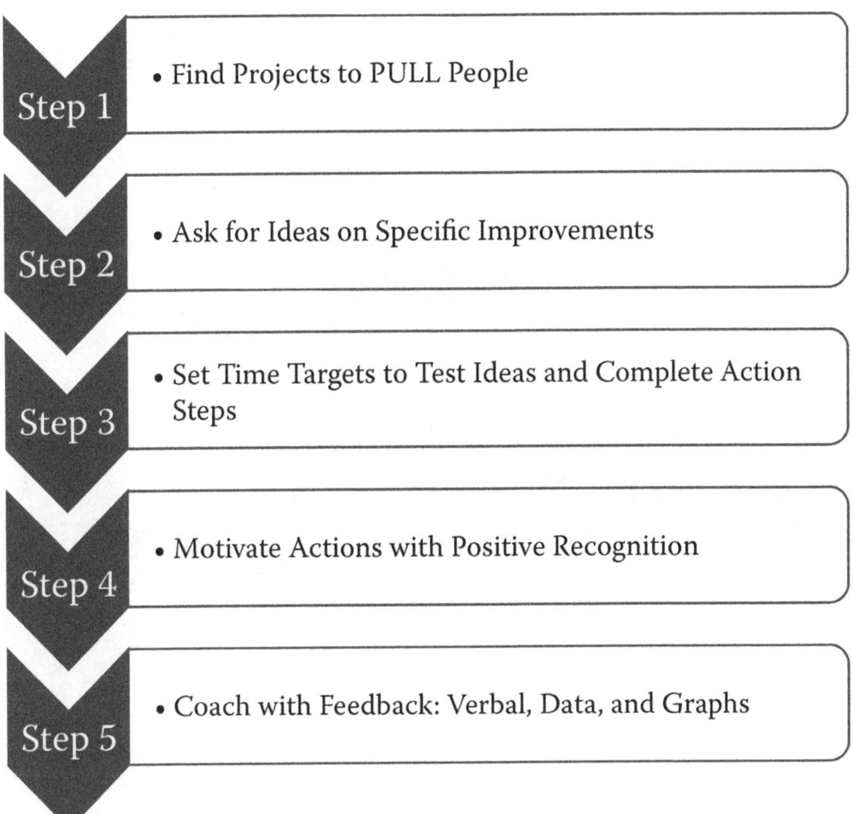

These five steps provide the tools you can use to quickly, easily, and effectively engage, involve, and motivate individuals. Then repeat with additional people. You'll be spreading engagement. Now let's get started by checking to see where you are now.

Roadmap on Your Journey to Results through Engagement

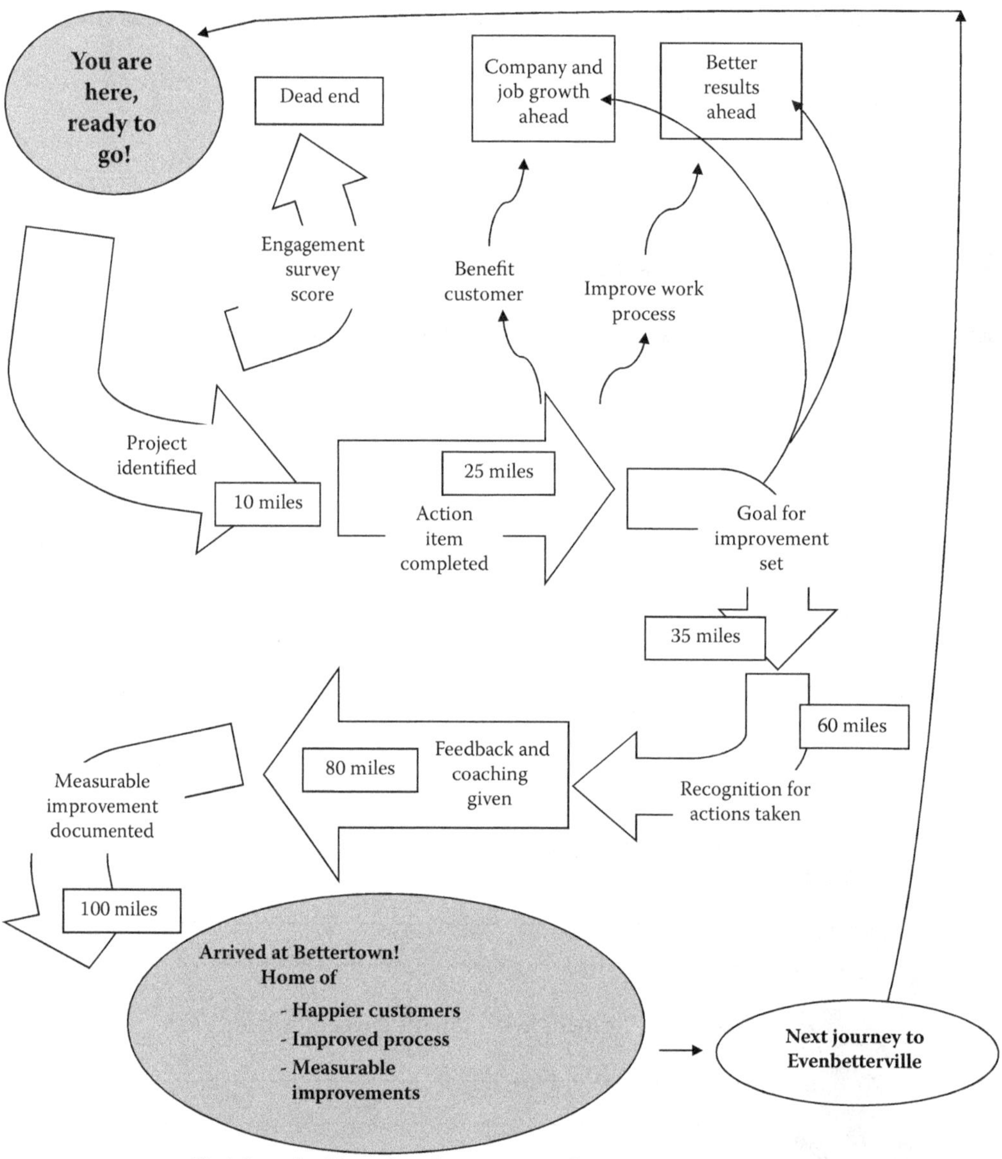

Quick quiz: How far along are you?

Check Off Your Progress on Your Engagement/Involvement Journey ... the First 100 Miles

Mark the Miles on Your Engagement Journey: Actions Completed (document your actions and circle your miles earned)				
		Date Completed	*By Whom*	*Miles Earned*
1.	Project identified			10
2.	One person has completed one action item to get the project started (repeat to involve more people)			15
3.	Goal for improvement is set			15
4.	Feedback and coaching given			20
5.	Positive recognition given to individual(s)			20
6.	Improvement measured and documented			20
			Total miles	

Chapter 4

Find Projects to PULL People

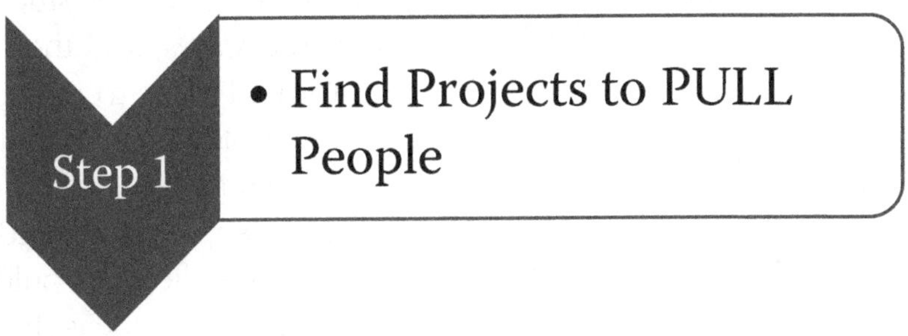

Key Points

A. Find an improvement project. It will *PULL people* and their knowledge, experience, skills, and interest.
B. What projects? Look at your organization's quality and delivery goals and your customers' needs.
C. How? Go to the workplace and look for things to improve. Ask your employees what they SEE that needs improvement (these are potential projects).

A. Find an Improvement Project. It Will *PULL People* and Their Knowledge, Experience, Skills, and Interest

How to engage people? Projects! Projects pull people!
Projects can be implemented

1. Formally or informally
2. By a group or by individuals

3. As a response to a request, a problem to solve, or a measurable goal
4. Initiated by an individual—"FIND and FIX"

B. What Projects? Look at Your Organization's Quality and Delivery Goals and Your Customers' Needs

Here's a project that was chosen at a New York DMV office, based on customer complaints about long wait times to get auto registrations and drivers' licenses. The project was to *Reduce Customer Waiting Time*.

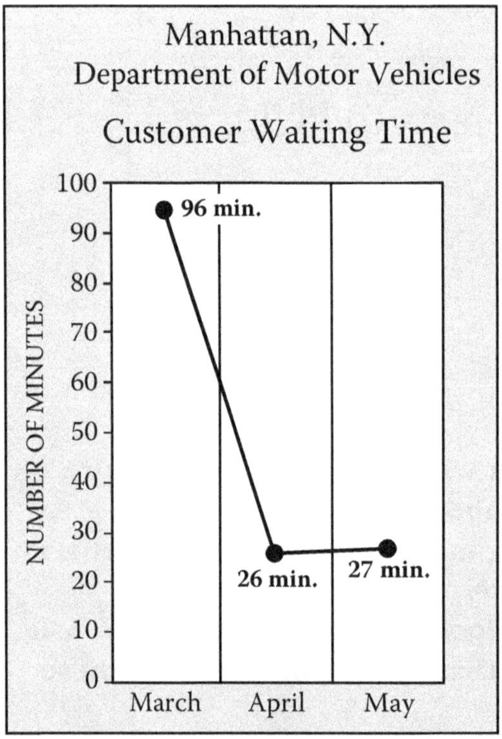

Once the project was agreed upon, office associates studied their current processes, and then they brainstormed ideas to make the processes faster while maintaining accuracy. They thought of actions for employees, supervisors, and managers that they believed would help. After testing these ideas, here's what they did:

- Created express lines for "post-card" renewals, so those customers wouldn't have to wait in line with people whose renewals took more time and documentation.
- Posted new process actions on the bulletin board to educate and remind everyone in the office of the new process to follow.
- Employees, supervisors, and managers gave positive recognition to each other when they saw anyone doing the new actions. Everyone was "in it together." Everyone could post "Seals of Approval" on the bulletin board next to the ideas they found helpful; that is, an idea that reduced the time to do their part of the process. The idea-originators' names were written next to the ideas they had contributed, so they had the satisfaction of those "likes" each time they looked at the board. Results: Average customer waiting time was reduced from 96 to 27 minutes in two months!

Where to begin with engagement and involvement? We can't do everything at once; we must start somewhere. (Albert Einstein famously said: "The reason God invented time is so that everything doesn't happen at once.") The following are some tools you and your employees can use to decide where to start.

Every work group has goals. It's whatever the organization pays that work group to produce. Types of goals are

- **Quantity**: Production schedule met (just-in-time)
- **Quality of work**: Conformance to specifications/customer requirements
- **Cost**: Cycle time, materials, labor
- **Timeliness**: Delivery on schedule or response time to requests or problems
- **Customer service**: Delivering to your customers and helping them solve problems
- **Safety**: Safe behaviors that create safe results (process improvement thinking, applied to safety)
- **Process improvement**: Reduction of cycle time and eliminating unnecessary steps (the Seven Traditional Wastes of Lean*)

All the goals listed are easy to measure, and most organizations focus their efforts around these key results daily and hourly. Many organizations have performance boards with graphs that show measurable goals and real-time performance.

You already know which of your business goals need to be emphasized; they're the ones where you're not meeting expectations and/or the ones you're asked about frequently. You also see and hear about problems with your work process. Ask your teams to help solve these problems and reach those goals—that's engagement!

Training his new engineers, Taiichi Ohno (considered to be the father of the Toyota Production System), drew a chalk circle on the production floor. He told the engineers, "Stand in this circle until you can see something to improve." He was teaching them to observe closely.

You don't necessarily need to stand inside a chalk circle, but Ohno makes the point that observing (really looking at what's going on around you) will present

* Seven Traditional Wastes of Lean: What we aim to reduce or eliminate—waste in transport, inventory, motion, waiting, overprocessing, overproduction, and defects.

a wealth of ideas for things that can be improved. As the baseball legend (and famous Lean Sensei) Yogi Berra said, "You can observe a lot by watching."

> "You can observe a lot by watching."
>
> Yogi Berra

Set Goals and Subgoals	
Engaging and Involving Employees with Purpose	
 **Wrong Way**	"You can't measure what we do. We just respond to 'fires.' Every day is different."
 **Right Way**	"This graph shows that our on-time delivery for the month is 79%. Our customers want 100%. Since we're a ways from there, let's look for ways to improve our process. Let's set subgoals for the next four months that will bring us up to 100%."

LOOK FOR THINGS TO IMPROVE: A CHECKLIST

- What slows you down?
- What gets in your way?
- When/where do you have to do extra walking?
- When does something go wrong?
- Where are the bottlenecks?
- Where are there stacks of WIP (work in process) waiting to be processed?
- People reaching or stretching more than an arm's length for tools or material. People bending or squatting to do the work.
- People waiting for a machine to finish processing a part.
- People waiting for parts, tools, material, or WIP.
- People repairing or reworking a part that has already gone through the process.
- Customers are complaining about something.
- Customers are asking for something.

WHEN YOU **SEE** ANY OF THESE THINGS, YOU HAVE A POTENTIAL PROJECT. AIM TO

- Reduce it.
- Eliminate it.
- Cut out an extra step.
- Make it easier to do.
- Make it safer to do.
- Change the process to make a good part the first time.
- Reduce the amount of walking needed to do the task.
- Redistribute the workload among operators so that WIP does not "pile up" at one workstation.
- Redistribute the workload (level loading) so that no one operator has to strain to keep up.
- Rearrange the workstation so that no strain (stretching, bending, or squatting) is necessary to do the task.

(See Appendix IV for a checklist of these steps.)

When you have a list of issues from the previous questions, select one issue using these criteria:

Goal: Pick a project to start on. With your employee(s), prioritize your list. If "yes," make a check mark below.				
Project Idea List	Biggest Problem?*	Helps work flow?	Helps customers?	We can do it ourselves?
Suggestion: Start with the one with the most checks				

* Exception to biggest problem rule: If you and your employee(s) are new to group problem solving, then pick an easy problem that can be solved in one or two weeks.

When you've selected one from this list, you're ready to invite one or more employees or coworkers to join your project team. Early wins build confidence and morale. Then you can gradually move to bigger problems.

Now, using a product concept you'll be familiar with, here is the first of 10 Engagement WD-40 Tips that will help you "keep everything moving freely." We use the WD-40 comparison (with thanks to the WD-40 Company for their permission) because WD-40 makes things move, makes things work, and makes life easier. These tips will, too.

Engagement WD-40 Tip #1

Ask employees to go see how the work could be made easier.

This is PULL and avoids the PUSH of "telling." Projects PULL people.

Use Engagement WD-40:

It keeps everything moving freely!

Projects PULL People's

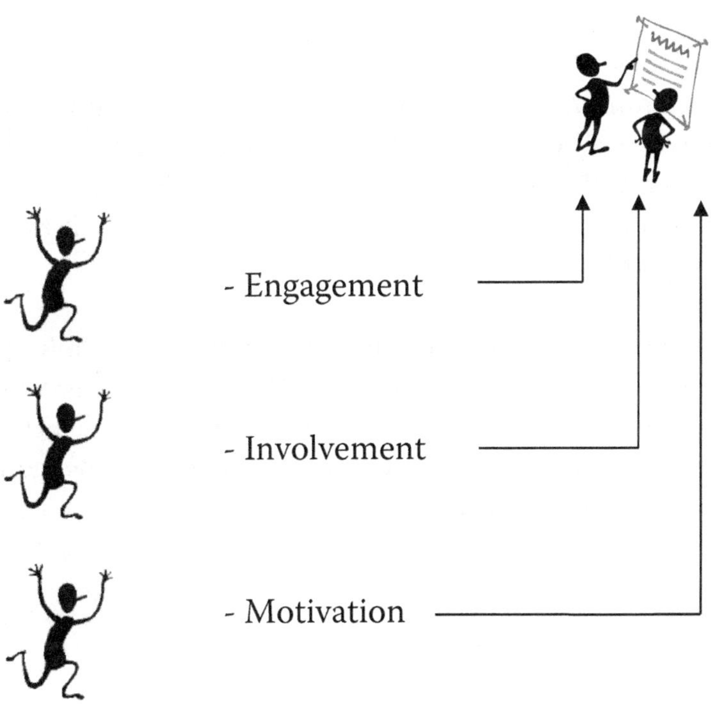

C. How? Go to the Workplace and Look for Things to Improve. Ask Your Employees What They SEE That Needs Improvement (These Are Potential Projects)

Here are four ways you can get this engagement:

1. *Kaizen process improvement events* with a group of people. Kaizen events are held over three to five days and begin with a half-day of training to learn Lean tools. But you don't have to wait for formal training or dedicated kaizen event teams or projects—the next three options work well and quickly.
2. *Projects* can include a small team working on a project over a longer period of time, concurrent with performing its regular jobs.
3. *Daily kaizen* is when a leader sets aside some time during the workday for everyone to make small improvements. For an excellent example of this, see the book and YouTube videos *2 Second Lean* by Paul Akers. Paul Akers owns FastCap LLC, a multimillion dollar company that manufactures tools for the cabinetmaking industry and launches ***20 new products each year***. He sets aside one hour at the beginning of each workday for his employees to work on improvements. They don't have to write a project plan, they just do it. Most of the innovations and improvements are made by individuals, not teams.
4. *Individual initiative* (FIND and FIX) can happen many times a day as your employees become self-starters. Think of the truck driver who put chains on his pickup truck to make deliveries on time. Think of the operator at the cathode-ray tube plant who knew how to solve the moisture problem.

You don't have to have formal training or a kaizen event to engage and involve your employees. Just ask them to FIND problems, recognize them for their ideas, give them permission to implement their ideas (FIX the problem), and recognize them for that action. The more you engage people, the more engagement you will get.

FIND and FIX

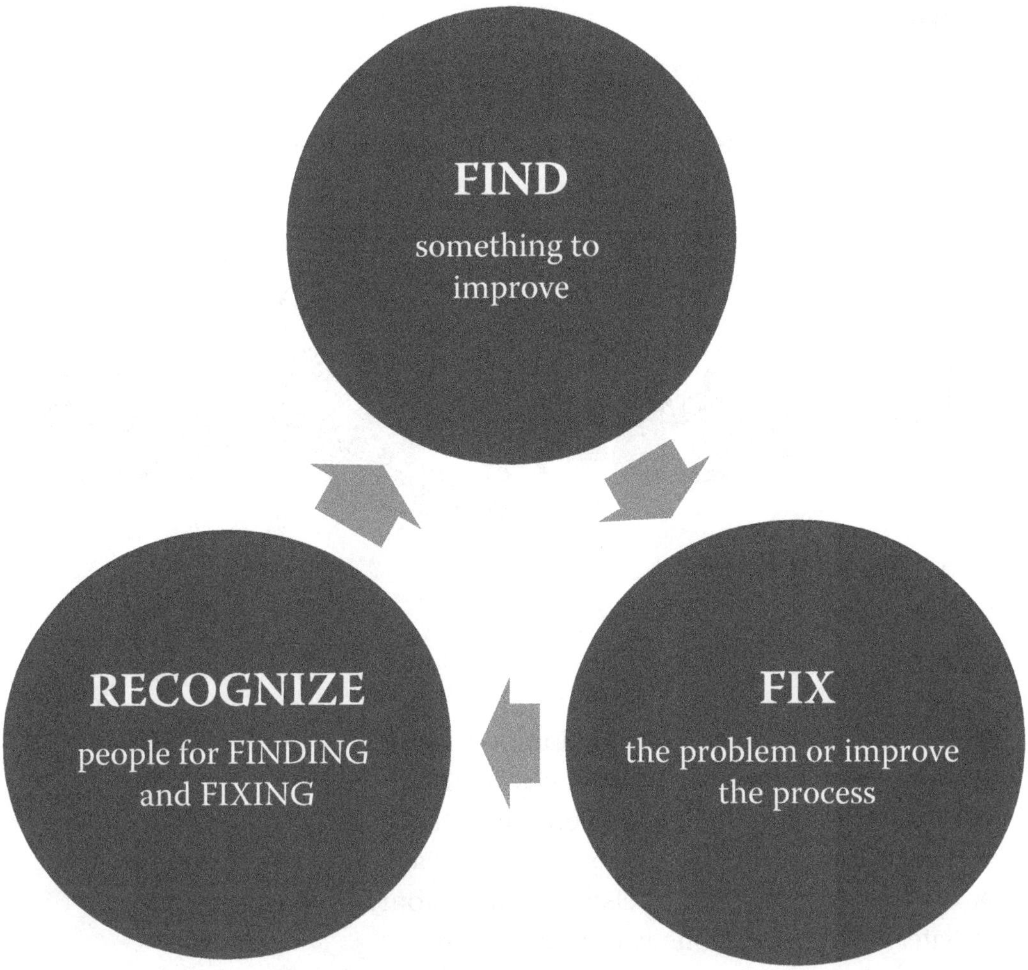

The more you engage people, the more engagement you will get.

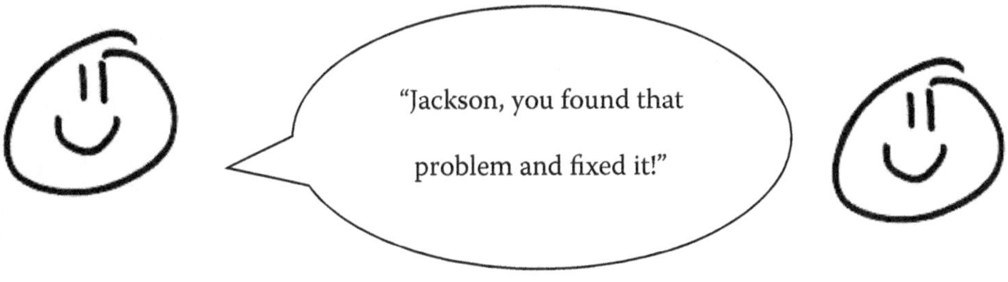

How to find a project? Walk the floor. See for yourself. Look for anything that is slowing or stopping the FLOW of production. Ask your employees what they see.

Where do you see FLOW bottlenecked?

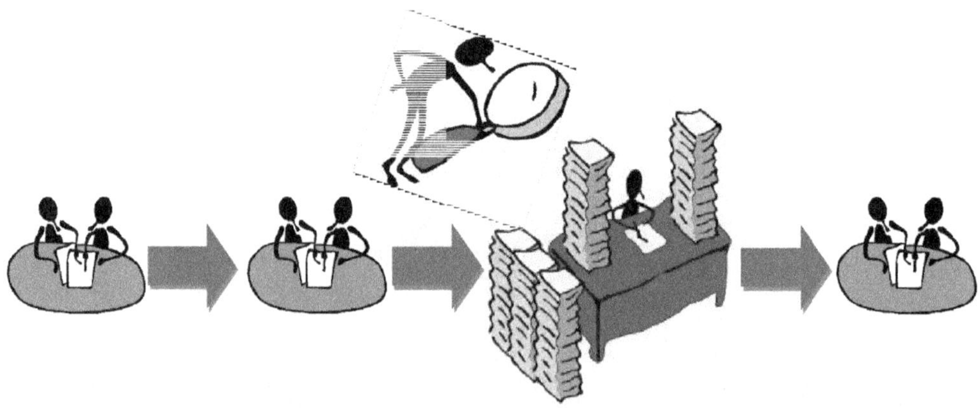

- Production: Where is production flow slowed or bottlenecked?
- Delivery: What part of the process makes us late?
- Quality: Where are defects being made?
- Timeliness: What causes customers to wait?
- Customer service: What else do our customers want from us?
- Safety: What situations lead to accidents?
- Cost: How can we reduce the cost of the product or service?
- Ease of Process: What frustrates you while doing your job?

Summary: Steps for Project PULL	
1. Find problems which you and your employees see in the workplace. Make a list and prioritize them.	
2. Pick a project to work on. Recruit individual(s) to work on it.	
3. Work with the individual(s) to solve the problem or complete the project.	

What's the Difference between PUSH and PULL?

Ever gone into a cell phone provider's store to get your broken phone fixed? You are being "pulled" in to get your problem solved.

What would happen if the store employee began trying to sell you a new phone, an expensive warranty, a more costly monthly plan, another phone for your spouse, and a tableful of accessories? None of this fixes your broken phone. This is "PUSH." This "PUSH" is how it can feel in the workplace when a manager or supervisor says, "Get involved," "Work as a team," or "Be more engaged." Employees wonder, "Be more engaged in WHAT?"

The effective leader will allow a project to PULL others in when she or he can show them how their work on the project will make their jobs easier, please customers, or beat the competition.

PUSH vs. PULL	
 **Wrong Way**	"I want you to get involved."
 **Right Way**	"Laurel, you know a lot about how we deliver to customers. Would you give me some ideas for how to improve our percent on-time service?"

QUIZ (answers on next page)	
1.	Find a project that _______ people. Don't _______ people.
2.	Ask your _______________, your ___________, and your _____________ what they SEE that needs improving.

(answers on next page)

ANSWERS TO QUIZ	
1.	PULLS . . . PUSH
2.	customers . . . supervisor . . . employees

Summary Checklist

- Find an improvement project. It will *PULL people* and their knowledge, experience, skills, and interest.
- What projects? Look at your organization's quality and delivery goals and your customers' needs.
- How? Go to the workplace and look for things to improve. Ask your employees what they SEE that needs improvement (these are potential projects).

Chapter 5

Ask for Ideas on Specific Improvements

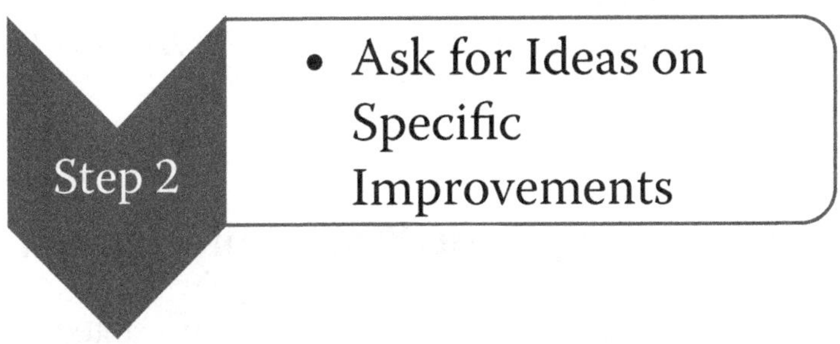

Key Points

A. Ask for help on a specific project or problem.
B. Accept ideas gratefully and acknowledge the people who gave them (even before determining if the ideas can be used).
C. Pick one to three ideas to test. Remember, your action here is to *select*, not to judge, criticize, or eliminate ideas.
D. Level the ideas so decisions can be made and/or actions can be taken immediately.

Definitions

Brainstorming: *A quick way to generate a large number of ideas. The brainstorming leader asks for ideas on a specific topic and records* **all** *ideas with no judgment.*

Leveling: *The process to determine whether ideas can be implemented or tested right away (Level 1), need approvals (Level 2), or need more information (Level 3).*

Janis's example

When I write a book chapter or design a training program, I print the draft and ask Mike (my husband, business partner, and coauthor) for additional ideas. He never fails to give me valuable input to make my product much better. When I see his new ideas and suggestions, I realize how much better the material will be for my customers.

Why is Mike so generous with his time and talent? Because I've learned (the hard way, of course) to receive his ideas gratefully.

A. Ask for Help on a Specific Project or Problem

In Step 1, you selected a specific issue for which you wanted help, from the categories of on-time delivery, quality, customer service, safety, or the work process. The next step is to ask for ideas to improve that issue.

Engagement WD-40 Tip #2: Specificity Succeeds

Specificity succeeds when we ask others for their ideas. Specificity gives them something concrete to respond to. Not, "How can we improve?" but, "How can we eliminate these burrs in the finished metal?"

Use Engagement WD-40:
It keeps everything moving freely!

For example, if the issue you've chosen is on-time delivery, tell the employee the reason for the need to improve. Tell him about your customers and their products or services to help him see the end result of his work. Tell him how these customers use the products or services he provides, and what happens when we don't deliver on time. For example, "Our customers use our blue painters' tape to make their home painting projects go faster and easier, with fewer touch-ups needed."

You want your employees to know they are "building a cathedral," not just "cutting stone." And you want to let them know how they can help. Ask them to help

a. Improve the process you use to produce your product or service
b. Suggest changes that will enable faster delivery

Share the Larger Goal and Ask for Ideas on a Specific Issue	
 **Wrong Way**	"How can we do better?" (not specific enough)
 **Right Way**	"Our new customer is growing fast and needs our products 100% on schedule. If we can deliver, we'll be able to grow with them. How can we reduce our cycle time?" (This zeroes in on one specific issue.)

Following the example here, write your plan for asking an employee for her ideas on a specific issue.

Step 1. Ask for ideas on specific improvements		
1. Ask for ideas on specific issues, sharing the details of your problem or challenge (don't go to an employee "empty-handed"—with a vague question or request).	For example, **say:** "Carter, I need your ideas for how we can eliminate these shipping errors."	**Not:** "Your opinion matters," or "Always feel free to give me your ideas." *These comments are not specific enough (these are lazy, one-time, "blanket" statements that will have little effect).*
Make a plan! Write your words for asking for specific ideas. Begin with the person's name*. 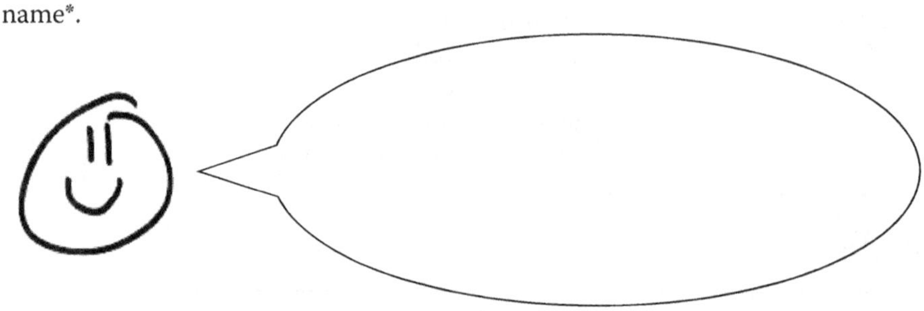		

2. When the person gives you ideas, take time to listen, understand what she gives you, and comment positively, right away. Ask her how we can test her idea.	Write your script for responding to an idea that an employee gives you. For example, "Carter, your idea could eliminate one source of errors. Let's set up a quick test tomorrow and see how it works." * Write your own script here. Begin with the person's name*.

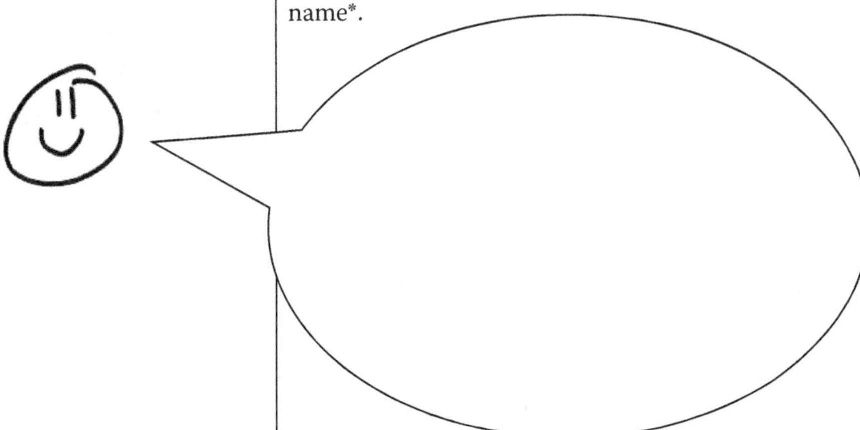

*Calling people by their names lets them know that you're focused solely on them and their ideas; it gets their attention and personalizes your communication. Use your employees' names often.

The following is a very quick way ("Trebek-ing") to comment positively when a person gives you a solution idea. Comments like these will "keep 'em coming," while criticism will "shut 'em down."

VERBAL UNDERLINING OR "TREBEK-ING"

(ALEX TREBEK-STYLE RECOGNITION)

Watching *Jeopardy*! we appreciate host Alex Trebek's quick, frequent, and punchy positive comments when contestants answer correctly.

For instance

"That's the river."
"She's the artist."
"He's the one."

To keep things moving quickly, Alex keeps his positive comments short. We call it verbal underlining: when you quickly acknowledge ("underline") what the person just said or did. It is useful for quick acknowledgment of someone's ideas, even before you know if the idea can be used. For instance

"That's a new idea, Molly."
"Let's test it, Luke."
"It's a possibility, Harry."

Just as when we underline a sentence in a book we're reading, this is a quick and easy way to say, "This is important."

"Trebek" 'em!

Challenge:
Play Jeopardy!: Watch Jeopardy! and jot down every comment Alex makes to let the contestants know they're correct. See how many different ones you can hear. You can use the same quick comments as recognition to your employees.

Daily Double: Write down six of your own quick "Trebeks" you can use when you see productive behaviors as you walk your department.

"Trebeks" for the Ideas Employees Give You	
1.	4.
2.	5.
3.	6.

Engagement WD-40 Tip #3

Use your employees' and coworkers' names often.

This reaffirms that your focus is on them and shows respect.

It gets their attention and paves the way for engagement.

Use Engagement WD-40:
It keeps everything moving freely!

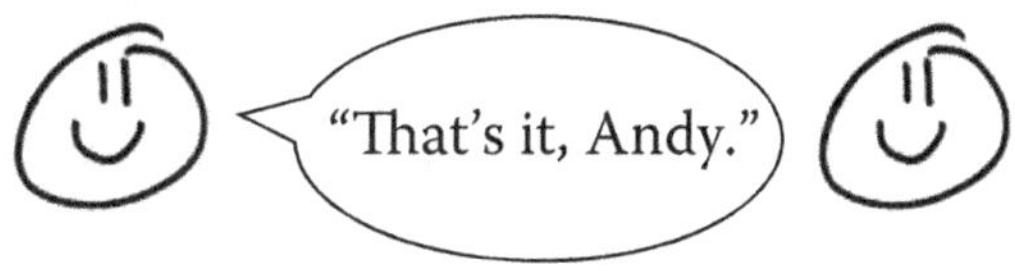

For Team Involvement

To meet your goals for on-time delivery, for example, ask for ideas from your group on how to improve your current process to reduce errors. The best tool for quickly getting group input is brainstorming. Ask your team members to take a turn leading as well. See Appendix V for a refresher on leading a successful brainstorming session, but the most important rule is to write down *all* ideas without criticism. You won't use them all, but you must write them all down if you want people to keep 'em coming.

B. Accept Ideas Gratefully and Acknowledge Them (Even before Determining if the Ideas Can Be Used)

Janis's story

In my example of asking for Mike's help, "gratefully" looks like this: I briefly read aloud his red-ink ideas when he gives me the pages he's edited (even if I'm busy at that moment), and comment positively on what I like. When I see something I'm not sure I'll use, I say, "That's a new angle," or "Tell me what you mean by this one," and listen carefully without comment. Of course, he would like it if I used all his ideas, but he lets go once he knows I've considered everything he's suggested.

I learned the hard way how to respond correctly. I can remember how I used to debate his ideas immediately when I saw or heard them, and even told him why some of them wouldn't work. (What was I thinking?!) You can guess how willing he was to give me suggestions after that! Fortunately, he was forgiving and responded with generosity when I figured out that I was punishing him with my negative comments, and I changed my evil ways!

ADDITIONAL WAYS TO ACCEPT AND RECOGNIZE IDEAS

Rephrase and allow him to explain further, or correct you if needed:

"So your idea is to ________________________________."

Then say, "That might work to increase/decrease/fix, etc.____________."

And, "How can we test it?"

Pinch Point Warning #2: You could "pinch" off your coworkers' flow of ideas with your negative comments. Then they'll stop giving you ideas. Instead, choose ideas to test.

C. Pick One to Three Ideas to Test. Remember, Your Action Here Is to *Select*, Not to Judge, Criticize, or Eliminate Ideas

There's no need for anyone to explain why any of the brainstormed ideas *won't* work. If you don't like some of the ideas, don't make negative comments about them. Just don't vote for them! ☺ Focus on the ideas you'd like to test.

Picking Ideas to Test

Ask your team to look at the sheet of brainstormed ideas. Give a marking pen to each person and tell them that they each have three "T's (for "test"). Ask each to write a "T" next to the ideas they want to test first. They can use all three of their "T's" on one idea, or two "T's" on one idea and the other on a different one, or spread their three "T's" to three different ideas. Circle the three ideas that get the most "T's."

Idea #1	Idea #2	Idea #3	Idea #4	Idea #5
T T T	T	T T T T	T T	T T T

When you've picked your three ideas, level them.

D. Level the Ideas So Decisions Can Be Made and/ or Actions Can Be Taken Immediately

Leveling is the process to determine whether the ideas

1. *Can be tested right away without first getting approvals (Level 1)*
2. *Need approval from anyone else who would be affected (Level 2)*
3. *Need more information to determine if the idea is Level 1 or 2 (Level 3)*

Leveling: Place your selected ideas into one of these levels		
Level 1	I can implement this idea without informing or checking with anyone else	
Level 2	I need to check with someone else before testing this idea	
Level 3	I need more information before deciding whether it's Level 1 or Level 2	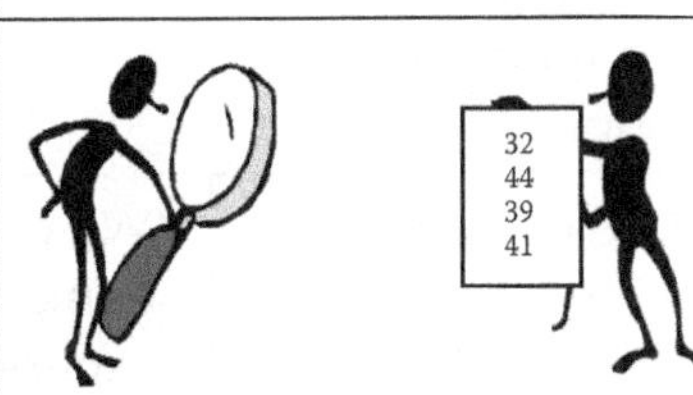

See Appendix VI for more information on leveling.

Write your action plans on a team log. Update and review it weekly or more often:

Team Log for _______________ (team)				
Date: __________ Project: __________				
Idea	Action Step	Volunteer	Target Date	Status

Summary: From Ideas to Implementation

Summarizing this chapter, here's your template for moving from ideas to making the ideas standard operating procedure (or standard work):

Checklist: From Ideas to Standard Work (Sample Project)	
1. Name the problem or project	"Our customers want delivery 100% to schedule. We're now at 76%."
2. Ask for ideas to solve or improve. Write down all ideas.	"How can we reduce our cycle time to reach this goal?"
3. Select one to three ideas to test	"We've brainstormed 11 ideas. Pick three to test that you think are most likely to help, based on your knowledge and experience. Write your "T's" next to the ideas you pick for testing."

4. Level those ideas	"Let's take these three ideas (which get the most T's) through the leveling template to decide which actions we can do right now. Then please volunteer for the action items you can take during the next week."
5. Log the activities	"Please write your action item, your name, and target date on our team log."
6. Evaluate, test, and decide whether to make this idea into standard work	"We'll review the log in one week and evaluate how our test worked. Based on that, we'll decide whether to make this idea part of our standard work."
7. Write the change into the standard work checklist	"Let's help each other make this change into a habit. Shawn, will you put a reminder sign at the work station? Each day let's all point and *give positive recognition* when we see someone using the new procedure. And remind each other if we forget. Let's do this for three weeks—agreed?"*

* For more information on building new standard work into a habit, see the book *Sustain Your Gains* by Michael McCarthy.

QUIZ (answers on next page)	
1.	We get more useful ideas when we ask about a ____________ issue.
2.	Use your employees' ____________ often to reaffirm your focus on them and respect for them.

ANSWERS TO QUIZ	
1.	specific
2.	names

Summary Checklist

- Ask for help on a specific project or problem.
- Accept ideas gratefully and acknowledge the person who gave them (even before determining if the ideas can be used).
- Pick one to three ideas to test. Remember, your action here is to *select*, not to judge, criticize, or eliminate ideas.
- Level the ideas so decisions can be made and/or actions can be taken immediately.

Chapter 6

Set Time Targets to Test Ideas and Complete Action Steps

Step 3

- Set Time Targets to Test Ideas and Complete Action Steps

Key Points

A. Set time targets for testing ideas and completing action steps.
B. Coach individuals to help them perform their project action steps.
C. Recognize people for completing their action steps on the project.

Definitions

***Time goal**: The target date to complete an action step*
***Coach:** Help someone learn a behavior that will help him or her become more successful; help develop a skill*
***Recognition**: Acknowledging a person for his or her actions, causing him or her to want to repeat those actions*

A. Set Time Targets for Testing Ideas and Completing Action Steps

A project log is useful for keeping track of ideas, action steps, and target dates. Example

Department: ***Production*** **Measurable Goal:** ***Reduce cycle time by 10%***			
Idea to Test	*Action Steps*	*Start Testing*	*Complete Testing/ Action Step*
Store parts at point of use.	1. Stage needed parts at individual work stations.	June 1	June 30
	2. Create 5S labels for each parts bin.	June 2	
	3. Calculate kanban cards for reordering parts from suppliers.	June 4	

B. Coach Individuals to Help Them Perform Their Project Action Steps

Once you've determined your project, coach for individual behaviors and skills to help team members complete action steps. The result of coaching is that people accomplish the project steps and gain skills as they do. They will acquire skills such as

- Technical skills: Doing something with their hands, using software, hardware, making calculations, or using tools or machinery
- Decision-making skills: Using criteria to select the right choice for the project (learning from incorrect choices and knowing when to consult someone else)
- Problem-solving skills: Taking initiative to fix problems, or beginning the process to fix, without pointing fingers of blame and without stepping away as if it's someone else's responsibility
- Leadership skills: Acting first and asking others to help; choosing a constructive direction for action
- Communication skills: Respectfully asking others for help, leading teams, asking diagnostic questions and listening carefully to the answers, making presentations, or representing the department to other parts of the organization or to customers

USING QUESTIONS: THE SOCRATIC METHOD

The Greek philosopher Socrates was famous for asking questions. He knew that you don't need to know all the answers, just how to ask questions in a way that helps other people learn (or realize how much they know).

You can use the Socratic Method by asking questions:

1. To find out what your employee already knows
2. To make *him* aware of what he already knows
3. To identify what else he needs to find out

Your questions will help him learn, feel good about how much he already knows, and develop more self-confidence. This will help you to be an effective coach.

Example: "Chuck, you are the one who pointed out these defects.

How can you and I find out what part of the process is causing them?"

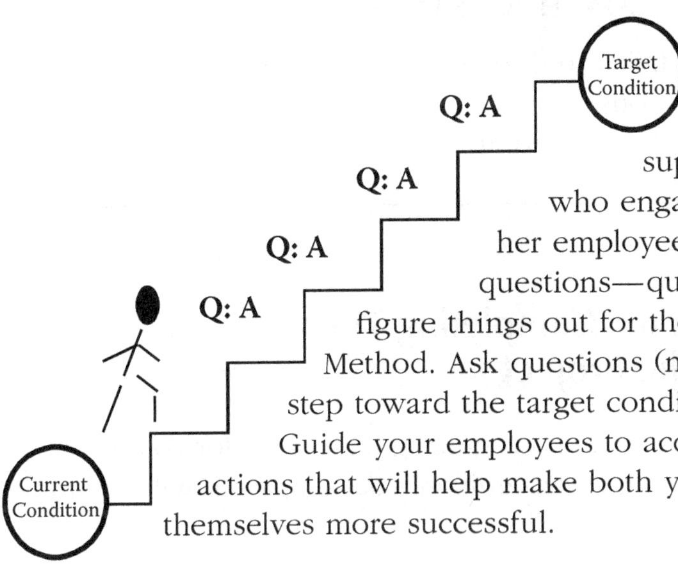

The Toyota Coaching Kata* focuses on the supervisor as a coach who engages and involves her employees by asking them questions—questions to help them figure things out for themselves—the Socratic Method. Ask questions (notice the Q:A on each step toward the target condition on this drawing). Guide your employees to acquire new skills and take actions that will help make both your department and themselves more successful.

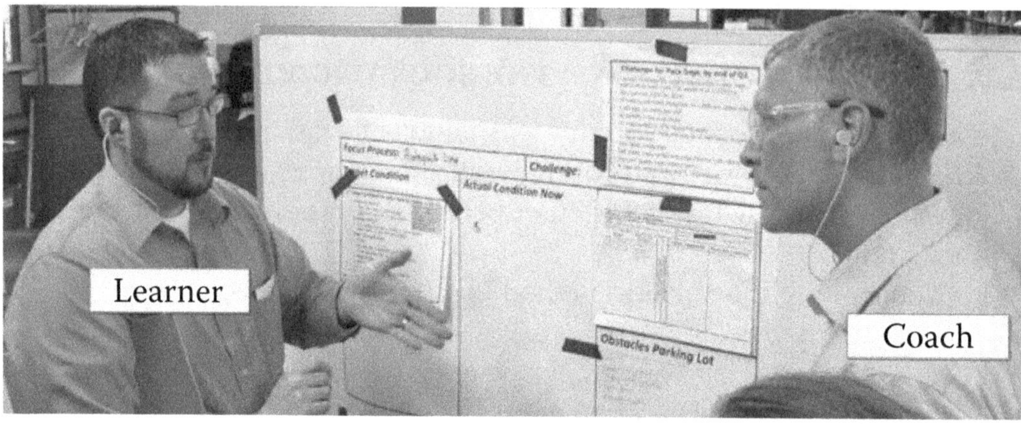

*In the photo from The Toyota Kata website by Mike Rother, notice that the learner (employee) is explaining his process to his coach (supervisor), rather than the other way around.**

Talking isn't teaching and listening isn't learning;
Talking is learning and listening is teaching.

Dr. Ralph Blackwood, University of Akron
(Mike's professor of Learning Theory)

COACHING STEPS

1. Ask the learner to talk you through the project steps.
2. Then you ask questions.
3. Let the learner do the answering.

C. Recognize People for Completing Their Action Steps on the Project

Here's a checklist for coaching and recognizing employees for completing their action steps. When you give recognition, your employee will *want* to do more!

* For more on this, see *Toyota Kata* by Mike Rother.

Checklist for Coaching and Recognition	
1.	Ask the employee what she needs to learn, or the tools or materials she needs to complete the action steps. Ask her if she already knows parts of it.
2.	Together, create a step-by-step plan for her behaviors to perform these substeps. Create a checklist showing these steps with target dates.
3.	Train her, or arrange for training if needed. Her training must include her actually *practicing* the skills, not just watching someone else do them ("my fingers"*).
4.	Ask her to mark her progress on the checklist and take the initiative to review it with you daily or every few days. (Ask her to come and show you her checklist without waiting for you to ask.) Ask her to set a schedule for this review and put the dates and times on both your calendars.
5.	Give her specific recognition (positive comments, notes, or both) for each step she completes. You've just helped someone get better at her job. She can now do something she was never able to do before. Yay!

*My fingers: We learn very little by watching another person perform an operation or reading a manual. Imagine learning to swim by watching another person swim or by reading about swimming. Effective learning occurs only when we perform the action (with our fingers). That includes using a computer keyboard . . . especially when using a computer keyboard!

Mike and Janis's story: "My Fingers"

When Janis asked Mike to teach her to do something on the computer, he would sit at the keyboard. Talking her through it, he would then stand and say, "Now you know how."

*But she didn't. The next time she asked for help on the same thing and he attempted to sit down at the keyboard, Janis said, "Let me sit at the keyboard—***my fingers***." (Janis realized she wasn't learning anything by watching Mike.)*

Mike talked her through each step but **she performed the steps**. *When they were finished, she knew how to do the operation and remembered it the next time.*

> **Tell** ***me and I will forget.***
>
> **Show** ***me, and I might remember.***
>
> **Involve** ***me with my hands and head, and I will understand, make it mine, and do it with enthusiasm.***

SAMPLE COACHING PLAN

	Steps for Coaching (and Recognition for Doing Project Steps)
1	 **You**: "Julie, what do you need in order to use this production software? Can you already use some parts of it?" "I know some of it. I plan to take online tutoring with practice to learn the rest."  **Julie**
2	"Great! Let's make a checklist for you."

	 **You** **Julie's Checklist to Master the Production Software** ☐ Complete the tutorial by ___________ (date) ☐ Work with (experienced user) Robert to get coaching by___________(date) ☐ Begin to use the software on ___________ (date) ☐ Discuss your progress with me on _________ _________ _________ (dates) ☐ Make a plan for continued practice and set goals on __________ (date)
3	 **You** "Julie, how can I help you complete this checklist?"
4	 **Julie** "You could ask Robert to make time for me. Thanks!"
5	 **You** "Sure. I'll talk to Robert and let you know. Also, would you put 10 minutes on both our calendars for us to review your checklist three times each week for a month?"

6	**Julie**	"Good idea. Can we put these times on our calendars right now?"
	Three Weeks Later	
7	**You**	"Julie, you've done everything on your checklist, and right on time. I'm proud that you've mastered it so well. You're helping us to serve our customers faster."
8	**Julie**	"Aw, shucks!" (big smile)

Option: You and your employee can create a graph to measure progress, shown here:

Coaching Plan for (name) ____________________ **Coach** ______________________

Skill Needed ____

1	Write in your steps to perform below, with dates. Fill in the box (make a bar graph) when achieved.

Steps to Complete the Project

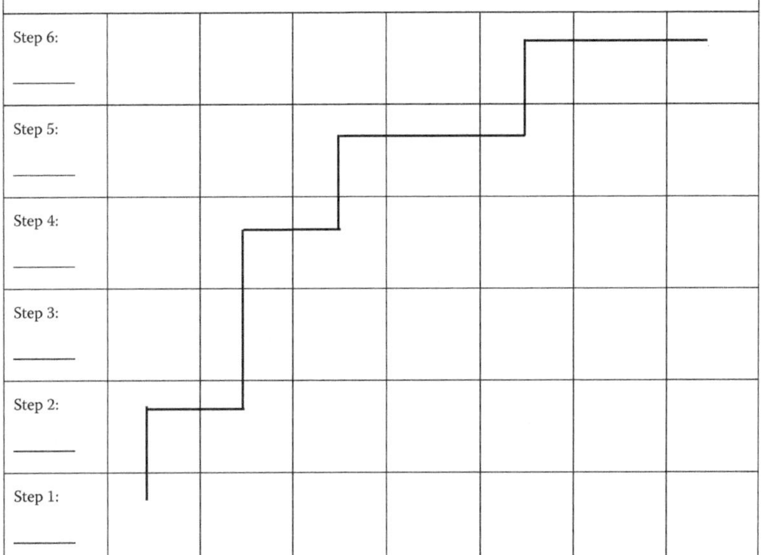

Dates: _____ _____ _____ _____ _____ _____ _____

2	Steps I can already do:
3	Steps where I'll need additional skills:
4	Training plan with dates:
5	Dates I'll review my progress with my coach:
6	Coach: Comments about progress

USEFUL PHRASES

- *"You can show me better than you can tell me. Let's go look."*
- *"You're making good progress."*

QUIZ (answers on next page)	
1.	Use the Socratic Method by asking the employee ________________.
2.	Talking is ________________ and listening is ________________.

ANSWERS TO QUIZ	
1.	questions
2.	learning . . . teaching

Summary Checklist

- Set time targets for testing ideas and completing action steps.
- Coach individuals to help them perform their project action steps.
- Recognize people for completing their action steps on the project.

Chapter 7

Motivate Actions with Positive Recognition

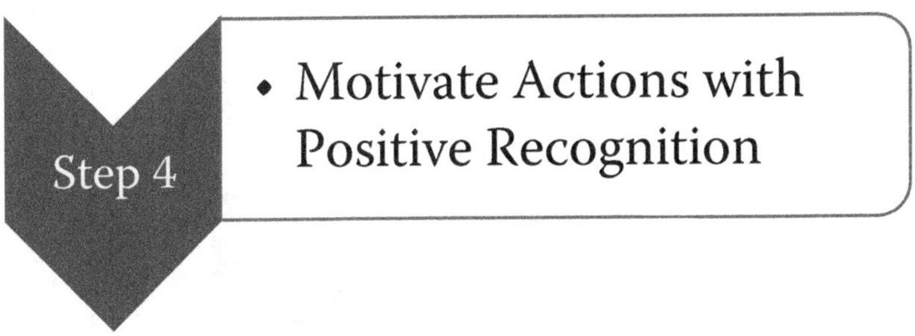

Applause is the accelerator.

Milliken & Company

Key Points

A. Give people a positive reason to get engaged.
B. Recognition is an action that shows respect for another person's effort or achievement. Recognition motivates ideas and actions.
C. Four ways to make your recognition effective and prevent unintended blunders
  a. Specific
  b. Stands alone
  c. Personalized
  d. Earned
D. People remember your words and actions to figure out what's acceptable and what's unacceptable; this creates your culture.

Definitions

Discretionary effort: *The time, work, and ideas that an employee gives* **above** *what it takes to "just get by" (or the minimum requirements of the job).*

Motivate: *To inspire a person to* **want** *to do something.*

Culture: *The actions and words in an organization for which people show approval or disapproval; often informal and not written down—"the way we do things around here."*

Proud Time: *To make time to recognize an individual's or team's accomplishments; can be initiated by either the person who wishes to share her or his accomplishment or by a leader or coworker.*

Here's an example of Proud Time:

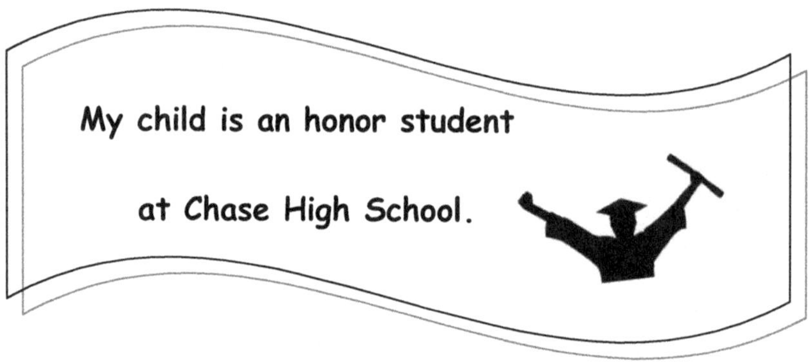

Celebration: *A gathering after an accomplishment to review our behaviors that made our success happen. We reminisce and tell stories about what we did to succeed—a "party" form of Proud Time.*

A. Give People a Positive Reason to Get Engaged

When you give positive recognition to individuals and teams, it strengthens the specific behaviors they have done to earn that recognition.

In the Safety Example, below, you can see the difference between the effort people will *voluntarily* make and the effort people "have to" make. The difference between the bottom trend line ("have to") and the top trend line ("want to") is their *discretionary effort*. This is the extra performance, the ideas, and the input you'll gain when you use positive recognition to motivate individuals and teams.

Safety Example:

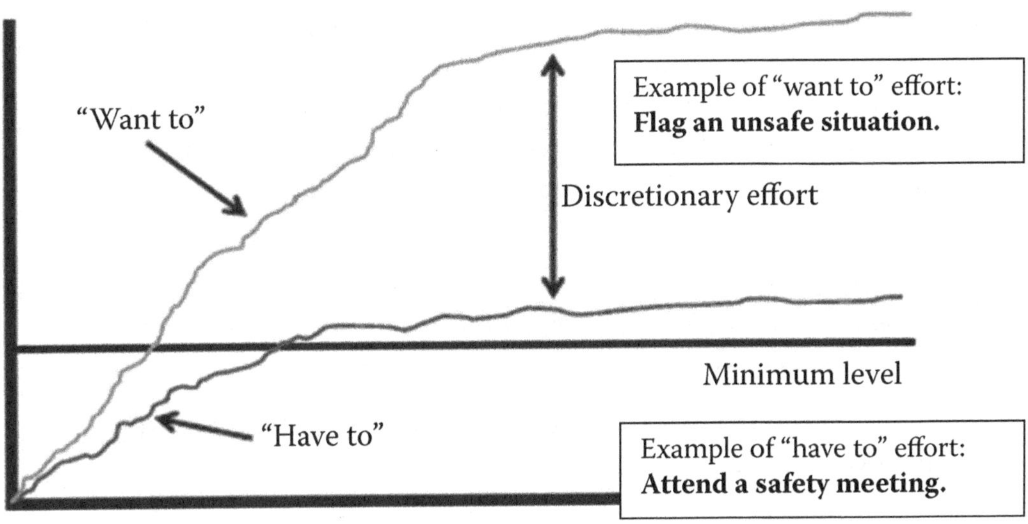

The Difference between "Just Enough to Get By" and Discretionary Effort

B. Recognition Is an Action That Shows Respect for Another Person's Effort or Achievement. Recognition Motivates Ideas and Actions

> ***Recognition is an* action*, not an item.***
>
> Theresa Chambers, *Recognition Works*

Our suggestions for giving positive recognition here are for *your* actions—things you do or say that show respect for someone's effort or accomplishment. *Actions, not items*. More importantly, your sincere approval. Not just "appreciation" (as in "thank you") but approval ("I like what you did here."). You always have the ability to give recognition; you can say it on the spot when you observe productive behaviors. No need for a budget, arranging a ceremony, giving an item, or getting approval for formal means of recognition. Don't use items for recognition.

Some supervisors depend on the company's large supply of tangible items imprinted with the company's logo: mugs, key chains, flashlights, ball caps. In the short term, these items are novel and create interest. But they do not make people feel valued or appreciated.

Only words and actions can make people feel valued. Items can become expected, be taken for granted, and given for the wrong reasons. Ever heard, "Oh, we gave Daniel a mug, now we have to give Patty one." Arggghhh!

Anything you buy by the gross won't be motivating for very long.

Here are some good examples of meaningful and effective positive recognition that don't cost a dime:

1. Just say it: "You're doing that right, Jan," or "Dan, I see you're following the process. Good job."
2. E-mails that *name the behavior* you want to recognize.
3. Positive notes on reports or graphs.
4. Recognition of individuals in meetings (first, find out if she likes to be recognized in front of others—not everyone does).
5. Give someone an opportunity to learn a new skill if you know that he would like it. Be sure to tell him what he did to *earn* this opportunity by naming his behavior that you like. Then he'll know what to continue doing.
6. Thumbs up or smile as you observe her working, or see the product of her work. Be sure she notices that you noticed.

Be sure she notices that you noticed—be "EPT"

E = Eye contact

P = Point to what the person is doing

T = Thumbs up

Be "EPT" (not "inept." Ha!)

C. Four Ways to Make Your Recognition Effective and Prevent Unintended Blunders

1. *When You Give Recognition, Be Very Specific about What You're Recognizing*

Not "Thank you," or "You always do a good job," but, "Kayla, your correct analysis saved me hours of work (*point to her analysis*). Now I can fix the right problem. You're a valuable help."

Use the "point-to" test:

If you can't point to what the person did, you're not being specific enough.

Template for Giving Positive Recognition

Start by calling the person's name: ______________________

Name her *specific* behavior that *you* value (say "I," not "we" or "the company"):

____

"Your action helps us because ______________________________

____."

We saw a video starkly showing the wrong way to give recognition. An actor was walking down a line of people shaking their hands and, in a monotone voice, saying, "Good job, fella. Acme appreciates it," sounding like a robot recording. When he came to a woman, he said, "Good job, fella. Acme appreciates it." At the end of this line was a life-size cardboard cutout of George Washington. He shook the president's cardboard hand and said, "Good job, fella. Acme appreciates it."

Having this silly image in our brains helps us remember to use "I," and name the specific behavior we like when telling someone we appreciate his or her work. The recognition comment should come from one human being to another, not from an impersonal company name or unspecified group.

Here are some sample cards you can fill out and deliver (in person if possible) to recognize any coworker. Just follow our template when you write your note.

You'll find blank forms like these in the back of this book, which you may copy.

bravo

Kayla, your correct analysis saved me hours of work. Now I can fix the right problem—a valuable help.

Jack

To: Laura

I like the fact that you . . .

. . . took the time to test your idea for improving our delivery time. Your data helps us speed up deliveries to our customers.

From: *Theresa*

That's how quick and easy it is to give positive recognition, a powerful tool for leaders.

Even with good intentions, most of us make mistakes when attempting to give positive recognition. One of the easy-to-make mistakes is failing to be specific about the behavior or results you want to recognize. The more specifically you communicate, the more likely the recipient is to know what he or she did well, and to accept your kudos with the feeling that you're sincere.

Give *Specific* Positive Recognition	
 **Wrong Way**	"Good job, everyone."
 **Right Way**	"Andy, the way you followed the new standard work helped us shave 10% off our cycle time."

2. Let Your Recognition Stand Alone

Don't be tempted to use your "recognition" conversation to give the individual more work to do or a higher goal to reach, or to talk about unrelated matters. Tell him specifically what you value, then close your mouth and go away. Come back later to handle these other issues. To get the maximum impact from your recognition, give the receiver time to soak it in (or "waller in it" as we say in the mountains) without jumping to another topic, or forcing him to hear something negative at this moment. (*Note:* Some management courses recommend mixing positive and negative comments. They're wrong!)

Pinch Point Warning #3: When you give positive recognition, let it stand alone. Don't follow it by talking about more work or a higher goal. For example, "Darren, you've reached your goal of 80% production. But your quality still needs improvement." Give your positive recognition and STOP. This will give your positive recognition time to sink in and have maximum effect. Handle new goals or needs for improvement at a *different time*. And **no buts!**

3. Personalize Your Recognition in Two Ways

- Start by calling the person by name. This helps both of you focus and block out all the other distractions that are always handy. And it tells the person that all your attention is on him at this moment.
- Also personalize your recognition by giving him the type of attention that he would find pleasing. For example, some people like to be recognized in a group. Some people hate that, and will respond much better to a private, quiet mention.

Everyone would like a fancy dinner as recognition—right?

Wrong!

When leaders realized that Fred had not missed a day of work in 22 years, they planned an awards banquet for him and others with good records. They sent Fred and his wife an engraved invitation to the banquet, stating that a chauffeured limousine would pick them up and that they would be sitting at the head table with the vice president as the special honorees.

On the morning of the banquet, Fred called in sick. No one had thought to ask him if he **liked** *public recognition. What a shame that he missed a day of work and ruined his record—just to avoid the fancy dinner.*

It's easy to find out the kind of recognition your employees like and don't like. Just ask them! For instance, "Erica, when I want to give you recognition for your good work, would you prefer that I do it in a meeting or in private?"

4. *Give Positive Recognition for Specific* Earned *Actions, Not Just to Be Nice*

Don't confuse giving recognition with adding benefits for all employees: celebrating birthdays, letting people bring their dogs to work, bringing in pizza because it's Friday, or other "being a nice place to work" actions. There's nothing wrong with doing these things, it's just that they don't have the effect of increasing specific productive behaviors like you might wish. Also, don't use "recognition" items as a bribe, as in this example:

Janis's story

A maintenance supervisor came to me (then an HR Manager) on a Friday: "I'm going to ask andy to work this weekend. You got a pocket knife or anything I can give him?"

Another argggbhh!

Don't give items in advance to persuade employees to take certain actions. This is bribery. If it's not earned, it's not recognition. Use recognition for specific actions that people *have already done*. It strengthens and increases these desired behaviors because they know how important those behaviors are to you.

If it's not earned, it's not recognition.

Give Credit and Positive Recognition for Specific Good Work	
 **Wrong Way**	"You're great, Kit."
 **Right Way**	"Kit, your idea for improving our testing has now shaved an hour off every transaction. You've helped us make our customers happier!"

D. People Remember Your Words and Actions to Figure Out What's Acceptable and What's Unacceptable; This Creates Your Culture

People can be motivated to take the actions we want them to take with negative means (threats of losing their jobs, demotions, or reprimands). But this isn't the kind of work culture we want, because negative motivators don't produce optimum performance or engagement. In a culture of fear, many humans will do just enough to get by, that is, just enough to keep their jobs or avoid the negatives for a limited time, but many will be looking for another job. They certainly won't be giving that "want to" discretionary effort described early in this chapter.

Your positive recognition creates the opposite culture: engaged, involved, and motivated.

THE FINE POINTS OF GIVING PROUD TIME

What is "Proud Time?"

It's when you tell someone "I'm proud of your achievement. Would you tell me how you did it?" Then you listen without commenting about how he could have done it better (that would only make him feel bad, not good).

If coaching is needed, do it later. Proud time is just for expressing pride in achievement and nothing else.

Also, ask your employees to let you know when *they* want Proud Time. Let them know you'd appreciate them telling you, "Please come over here—I have something I'm proud of. I'd like to show you."

Labeling a conversation "Proud Time" signals "this is positive recognition time, not problem-solving time." It can be initiated by the leader or the employee. When you make Proud Time a part of your culture, you'll start seeing more and more things and people to be proud of.

Proud Time in Everyday Life

You noticed the bumper sticker earlier in this chapter: "My child is an honor student." The parent who puts it on his car is proud of his son's grades, and is inviting "Proud Time" by displaying the bumper sticker. Other people will make positive comments to him. He will repeat these comments to his son. The son hears about other people's approval of his accomplishment. That family is building a culture of pride in achievement. You can build the same at work.

Celebrations

Hold a celebration for a team within three days after the team has achieved a goal. Refreshments always add to the fun, but the primary purpose is to reminisce and review all the actions of the team that helped achieve the goal. Good coaches do this for Little League or soccer teams. They go out for pizza and talk about who caught a fly ball or who blocked a goal.

At work, the leader can start by naming a few actions, and then invite others to join in to name additional actions they saw.

Celebrations have three important benefits:

1. The team is reminded of the actions that created success, and will continue to do them.
2. When someone names a positive action of his coworker, that's recognition to the person who did that action.
3. Getting into the habit of noticing and naming coworkers' positive actions creates a positive culture of achievement and teamwork.

To get the most from your celebration, lead the discussion of these actions *before you bring in the food*. Once folks see and smell the food, it's tempting to shorten the discussion and tear into the food. We're all human (and hungry)! Don't let the arrival of the food upstage the real reason for the celebration—to reminisce and recognize your team's success.

1. Schedule your celebration at 11:00 to discuss your success.
2. Then bring in the food at 11:20.

Engagement WD-40 Tip #4

Use EPT for quick recognition in the Gemba (workplace)

 Eye contact

 Point to what the person is doing

 Thumbs up

Use Engagement WD-40:

It keeps everything moving freely!

QUIZ (answers on next page)	
1.	Four ways to make your recognition effective and prevent unintended blunders are ____________, ____________, ____________, and ____________.
2.	EPT means ______ contact, ______ to what the person is doing, and ______ up.

ANSWERS TO QUIZ	
1.	specific . . . stands alone . . . personalized . . . earned
2.	eye . . . point . . . thumbs

Summary Checklist

- Give people a positive reason to get engaged.
- Give specific recognition by naming what the person did.
- Use these four ways to make your recognition effective and prevent unintended blunders:
  - Specific
  - Stands alone
  - Personalized
  - Earned
- Choose your actions with the awareness that your actions are creating your culture.

Chapter 8

Coach with Feedback: Verbal, Data, and Graphs

Step 5

- Coach with Feedback: Verbal, Data, and Graphs

The real question is … are you going to mark people's papers, or help them get an A?

Garry Ridge
CEO, WD-40 Company

Key Points

A. Tell and show people frequently (daily or twice a week) how they are making progress on the project, and what they can do to improve.
B. Coach employees to use graphs and checklists to track project progress.
C. Check your progress on results (% on-time delivery, etc.) from the date you made the process/project change.

Definitions

Baseline: *Measurement of past performance before your team makes changes. Baseline gives you something to compare your progress to, so you'll know if your changes are working.*

Communication: *Words, actions, body language, facial expressions, documents, and signs that send messages to other people.*

Feedback: *Information on performance that helps an individual know how to improve.*

Graph: *Data posted visually showing baseline, goal, and actual performance. Dots, lines, or bars show a trend over a time period.*

A. Tell and Show People Frequently (Daily or Twice a Week) How They Are Making Progress on the Project, and What They Can Do to Improve

On their wedding day, the crotchety old man said to his wife-to-be, "I'm telling you now that I love you. If anything ever changes, I'll let you know."

We know better than to try to get away with lazy "no-feedback" behavior like this if we want to motivate teams (or any kind of relationship). How well would a basketball player perform if there was no scoreboard to reflect her last basket? Or no game clock to show the time remaining in the game?

Feedback has the same importance for us in all our jobs. We want to know what we're doing well and where we need to improve.

> *Without feedback, no improvement is possible.*

Make feedback part of your work process. If there are graphs that don't serve as triggers to do something different in your process, get rid of them. They're wallpaper.

Too many performance boards become a hall of mirrors that don't give feedback because they don't trigger any different action.

Think of your trip to your haircutters. When he turns you to the mirror and says, "Take a look," he expects further direction or, "OK as is." Your feedback must past the haircutter's test: "Do something different," or "OK as is."

Coach and Give Frequent Feedback	
 **Wrong Way**	"I'll let you know if you mess up."
 **Right Way**	"Pat, let's make this graph so you can post the team's production every day. Please show me the data every Tuesday and Friday at 4:00. This will help us both know what to do to help our team reach the goal."

B. Coach Employees to Use Graphs and Checklists to Track Project Progress

Will your employees be fearful of the use of graphs? That depends. Were data and graphs used in the past to punish them or to give them positive recognition?

Mike's story demonstrates why employees can see graphs as a good thing:

> *After seeing her coworkers being recognized for their improvements shown on a graph, a woman who worked in the accounting department at Preston Trucking went to her supervisor and said, "Can I have a graph too? I measured myself."*

Graphs are more effective than reams of data. As we know, "a picture is worth a thousand words." Putting data on a graph shows a picture of performance in relation to the current state (baseline) and the goal. You can SEE your progress.

Coach your employees and teams to update their own graphs and bring them to show to you. This means they see their current performance even *before you do*. They can be thinking of ways to improve before they bring their graphs to you. They have literal ownership. This makes your coaching job easier:

- If the project graph shows improvement, ask your employees to tell you how they made the improvement. Listen without offering "better" ideas at this moment (you can come back later with coaching ideas if you want to). Compliment them for both their efforts (how they did it) and their results (data on the graph).
- If they aren't making progress, ask, "Any ideas to get closer to your goal?" Then listen. Give recognition for their ideas and tell them which ideas you'd like them to test. Or, if you don't think they're on the right track, you can offer suggestions for other actions they can take.

For Team Feedback

When it's a team project, have the individuals take turns updating the graph, but discuss the data and action plans with all of them. Here's how your team's graph might look:

Department X: On-time Delivery							
100%							**Goal**
98%					Subgoal		
96%				Subgoal			
94%			Subgoal				
92%		Subgoal					
90%	●						
Week Ending	1/6 (Baseline)	1/13	1/20	1/27	2/3	2/10	2/17

Pinch Point Warning #4: Keep your graphs up to date or take them down. Out-of-date graphs become wallpaper and teach team members to *ignore* what you post on performance boards.

C. Check Your Progress on Results (% On-Time Delivery, etc.) from the Date You Made the Process/Project Change

When you measure your results, if they haven't improved, go back to Step 2 and test a different idea. Remember that we are *testing* ideas to see if they produce improved results. If the results don't improve over the baseline, test a different idea.

Engagement WD-40 Tip #5

Coach employees in how to use graphs and checklists to track their own progress.

Use Engagement WD-40:

It keeps everything moving freely!

QUIZ (answers on next page)	
1.	In the case of feedback, no news is _____ good news.
2.	Without feedback, no _______________ is possible.

ANSWERS TO QUIZ	
1.	not
2.	improvement

Summary Checklist

- Tell and show people frequently (daily or twice a week) how they are making progress on the project, and what they can do to improve.
- Coach employees to use graphs and checklists to track own progress on their projects.
- Check your progress on results (% on-time delivery, etc.) from the date you made the process/project change. If the result hasn't improved, go back to Step 2 and test a different idea.

Chapter 9

Complete, Then Repeat

Congratulations!

When you have completed a project using the previous steps, you've engaged, involved, and motivated the members of that project team. It will now be easier to engage, involve, and motivate *more* people.

Why? Other people will see the success and fun their coworker or coworkers had. They'll now want to have some success and fun themselves. If they come to you asking to be involved, you know you've succeeded. If they come complaining that they weren't included, that's also good news. Don't make the mistake of saying, "Fine. Come to the next team meeting." Instead, say, "I'm glad you're interested. Give me your ideas for a project that would improve our process. How about let's talk tomorrow at nine?" This is a good springboard to launch the engagement of another individual.

This step is important because as you continue to replicate Project PULL, you're making a culture of engagement, involvement, and motivation. When you make it ongoing like this, none of your employees will ever question whether this is "the program of the month." Why? Because it never stops!

The tools in the following chapters are for fine-tuning, troubleshooting, and making your culture even more positive. You may want to pause at this point and use Chapters 4 through 8 to get your project started. Then come back to Chapters 9 through 16 when you need them.

Chapter 10

How Many People to Engage? Let the Project PULL the Number of People

Key Points

A. Start with your project, problem, or needed improvement.
B. Determine the type of general skills and specific "how-to" knowledge you'll need to work your project.
C. Recruit individual(s) who have these general skills and the specific "how-to" knowledge.
D. Engage the individual(s) by asking for their help. Build a team if needed, one person at a time. Use projects to PULL people.
E. Aim for four to six people on your team.

How do you eat an elephant?
One bite at a time.
How do you build a team?
One individual at a time.

Start by asking one individual to help you with a project or to improve a process. If you need more "how-to," find another individual who has it, then another. Before you know it, you'll have a project team.

A. Start with Your Project, Problem, or Needed Improvement

Do you want to

- Make production easier?
- Improve on-time delivery?
- Prevent defects?
- Decrease changeover time from one product to another?

In other words, let your project determine which employee(s) you ask for help.

B. Determine the Type of General Skills and Specific "How-to" Knowledge You'll Need to Work Your Project

Definitions

General Skills: *Skills that can be used in many situations: welding, spreadsheets, machining, computer programing, etc.*
Specific "how-to": *A skill specific to your work process, such as "how to assemble the latching mechanism."*

For example, who knows the current process, who can use the software, or who has performed the work? You may need three people who know these three things, not necessarily one individual who can do all three of them.

List the skills your project needs:

- General skills: ______________________________
- Specific "how-to" knowledge: ______________________________
- Has done the work steps: ______________________________

C. Recruit Individual(s) Who Have the General Skills and the Specific "How-to" Knowledge

You will want to pick people who you can make available for the time needed, in addition to having the general skills and specific "how-to" knowledge your project needs. You can use this checklist to help you decide.

Pick the Team! *Project:* ______			
Names of Individuals	Have Availability?	Have Needed Skill?	Have Needed Knowledge?

D. Engage the Individual(s) by Asking for Their Help. Build a Team if Needed, One Person at a Time. Use Projects to PULL People

When you ask a person for his help

1. Tell him why you want his help by naming the reasons you know his help will be valuable to you (you've just listed these reasons on the "Pick the Team!" table).
   For example
   > *"Don, I would like your help to do this test. You know what our customers want and need. I appreciated how you made sure that the last software conversion was customer friendly."*

2. Tell him the project you want his help with and the role and responsibility you have in mind for him.
   For example

   > *"Don, we average two days responding to customers. Customers have told us that our main competitor usually gets back to them the same day. We need to improve our process to give same-day service. I'd like to have your ideas. Are you willing to help?"*

If he says yes, ask, *"What do you need from me to get started?"* and then make a plan. Don is now *engaged*. When he begins taking actions, he's *involved*.

When you do this, you're using the PULL method. People will be "pulled in" based on the "demand" (need) for their help with a project or problem. Telling people their help is wanted and needed arouses their curiosity. This curiosity "pulls" them to begin tinkering with the project. (Saying "Let's have teams" without identifying the project idea is "push," and won't arouse curiosity or improve your work process.)

In the example with Don, you may soon need to involve additional people to

- Think of additional ways to improve the process
- Test ideas
- Use a skill that Don doesn't have

So just repeat the process of identifying your needs, selecting the individual, and asking for his or her help. You may create a team of only two. Let the needs of your project PULL the number of team members needed.

The Right Way to Build a Team: The *PULL* Method

1. Ask an individual to help you with ideas on a specific issue

2. And another who can help on this issue

3. And another

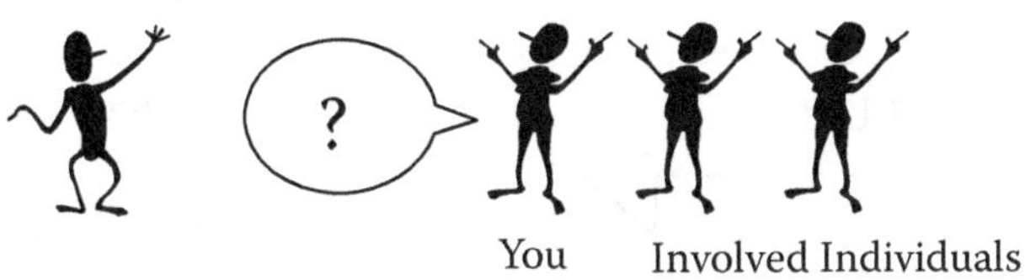

4. And another and another

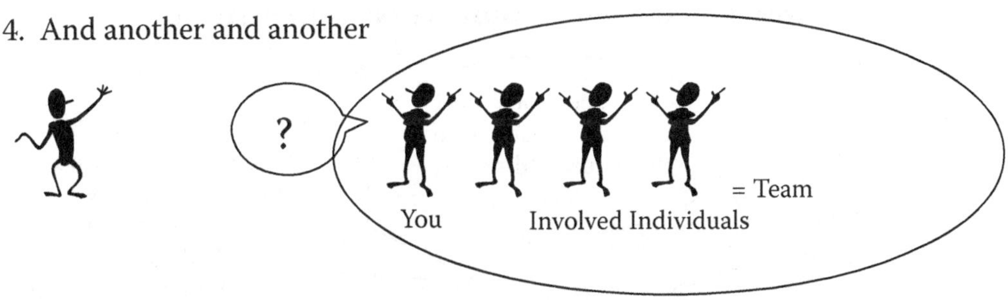

Pretty soon you have the team you need to work on a project or issue. You have shown them one-by-one that you value individuals' ideas and appreciate their extra efforts. In other words, the "engagement" habits between you and the team members are stronger. The next time you ask them to work on an issue or project together, their ideas, volunteering, and communication will come more easily and naturally.

The Wrong Way to Build a Team: The *PUSH* Method

Forming a team just for the sake of having a team is similar to the PUSH method in manufacturing, defined as *manufacturing products without a customer order*. In this scenario, the team members will lack the reason to work together as a team: a project. Without a project to work on, you are "pushing on a rope," trying to convince all of them that "teamwork" is a good idea. They may see this as a waste of time. So use PROJECTS to PULL instead.

Projects **PULL** **P**eople

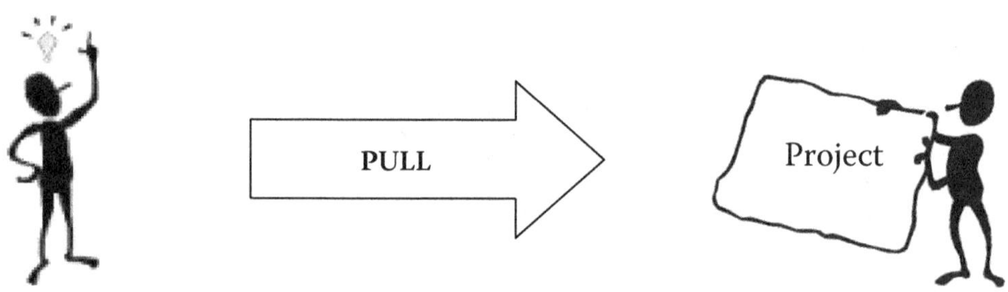

How Engagement "Snowballs" into a Team

Engagement WD-40 Tip #6

Build a team one person at a time. How? Invite them.

Use Engagement WD-40:

It keeps everything moving freely!

E. Aim for Four to Six People on Your Team

The ideal number for a team is four to six. This isn't a hard and fast number, but the criterion is "as many as you need to get the project done—no more." Two can be a team. If you form teams of 10 people, don't expect the project to move as fast.

In general

The larger the group, the longer everything takes.

Don't invite "everyone" just to avoid leaving someone out. Invite people based on your project's needs. If you skip someone, include them on a different project later. Let them know that's what you intend.

Pinch Point Warning #5: Putting people on the team without a job to do is asking for trouble. They will make a job for themselves—criticizing, whining, or blocking.

QUIZ (answers on next page)	
1.	____________ pull people.
2.	Engage individuals _____ -by- ______ to build an effective team.
3.	Asking people for their _________ is one of the best ways to motivate.

ANSWERS TO QUIZ	
1.	projects
2.	one . . . one
3.	ideas

Summary Checklist

- Start with your project, problem, or needed improvement.
- Determine the type of general skills and specific "how-to" knowledge you'll need to work your project.
- Recruit individual(s) who have these general skills and the specific "how-to" knowledge.
- Engage individual(s) by asking for their help. Build a team if needed, one person at a time. Use projects to PULL people.
- Aim for four to six people on your team, +/– two

Chapter 11

How Project Teams Create Motivation

Key Points

A. People are motivated by having their opinions valued.
B. People are motivated by being "in on things."
C. People are motivated by feeling part of a team.

When you engage and involve employees in project teams, three motivators "kick in":

A. People Are Motivated by Having Their Opinions Valued

When you ask employees for their ideas, it shows that you respect their experience and expertise. We all like to be shown respect. This may be the first time some employees have been shown the respect of someone asking for their ideas and opinions. Don't underestimate that.

B. People Are Motivated by Being "In on Things"

People like to be "in the know." When you show them data on customer satisfaction or the number of days your competitors take to fill an order, they feel that you trust them with this information. In other words, they'll feel respected as intelligent adults and valued in their roles. This helps them understand the need for improvements, and gives them a greater sense of ownership and belonging within the organization.

C. People Are Motivated by Feeling Part of a Team

When we're part of a team, we want to see our team win. When a group of people tackle a challenge to achieve a goal or overcome a threat (such as losing business due to a quality or delivery problem), the ideas of the group generate energy. The enthusiasm of individuals can be contagious, especially as the group members perceive that their ideas for improvement might work. As their work progresses, they enjoy each goal achieved and the feeling of accomplishment together. Camaraderie and fun become social recognition and add to the feeling of being included. Accomplishing a goal together creates unique memories, a bond of trust, and a feeling of connection and success. When the goal is reached or the improvement is made, they will point to it and say, "*We* did that!"

Think of a time when you were on a team or in a club at school: the basketball or soccer team, the yearbook staff, the photography club, or Future Farmers of America. How did you feel when your team played well, or your club's project succeeded?

That's exactly how your employees feel when they're part of a group that runs a successful project!

Look back at the three motivators listed at the start of the chapter; they look like privileges usually reserved for people at the higher levels in organizations. They are a natural part of being engaged and involved in useful work (process improvement and problem solving). When people experience these things, they'll be eager to participate the next time you ask.

Projects Pull Pride

When you have a few successful projects with your individuals and teams, it will get easier the next time. Why? They've learned through their experience with you that:

1. You're sincere in wanting their ideas.
2. You seriously consider their suggestions and give them feedback, whether their ideas are used or not.
3. You acknowledge and give them credit for their extra efforts.

This begins a "coaching" relationship of mutual respect. When you begin your efforts with a specific project and think of the individuals who can help on that project, you're like a basketball coach recruiting for talent.

3-SECOND ENGAGEMENT IN EVERYDAY CONVERSATION

"Let me know what you suggest."
"Come get me when you're ready to show me."
"You decide."

QUIZ (answers on next page)	
1.	When you engage employees in project teams, you demonstrate that you value their ____________.
2.	When you engage employees in project teams, they will enjoy and benefit from being ____ on __________.
3.	When you engage employees in project teams, they will feel part of a _______.

ANSWERS TO QUIZ	
1.	opinions
2.	in . . . things
3.	team

Summary Checklist

- Engage people to show that you value their opinions.
- Engage people to get them "in on things."
- Engage people to make them feel part of a team.

Chapter 12

Build a Culture of Trust with Your Actions

Key Points

A. Your actions as a leader can be trust-builders or trust-busters.
B. Tell the truth, even if it's difficult for both people in the conversation.
C. Do what you say you will do.
D. Never make negative statements about other employees. Tell them to their faces what you want them to improve.
E. Give credit where it's earned.

Definitions

Culture: *The actions and words in an organization for which people show approval or disapproval; often informal and not written down— "the way we do things around here"*

Trust: *Your experience that someone tells the truth; she will do what she says she will do; her actions match her words*

Communication: *Words, actions, body language, facial expressions, documents, and signs that send messages to other people*

A. Your Actions as a Leader Can Be Trust-builders or Trust-busters

Your actions and words serve, as others see you, to demonstrate that you will:

- Tell the truth.
- Do what you say you will do.
- Let each person be the *first* to know your opinion of his performance; always discuss issues about his performance *with him first*. Then, keep it private.
- Be quick to recognize the individual who has solved a problem, improved a process, or advanced a project.

B. Tell the Truth, Even If It's Difficult for Both People in the Conversation

Lane, a technical writer, was told by her supervisor, Ryan, that he was sending her to a communications seminar as positive recognition for her good writing on a recent project. Lane replied that she would rather not attend. Ryan replied, "Well, the truth is, I think you need to improve in how you communicate with your coworkers. I have a small budget, and I wanted to use this as both a way for you to improve and as recognition." It's certainly a good thing for a supervisor to arrange training for his employee, and training can be an effective and appreciated form of recognition **if** *it's something the employee wants. But for Ryan to pretend it was recognition was a trust-buster. He should have told Lane honestly what he wanted her to improve. Now she questions his sincerity on many other things he says. Though his intentions were good, his action was a trust-buster.*

It's difficult for many leaders to talk to their employees about improving their performance or skill deficiencies. However, most employees value honesty. They would rather hear the negative feedback straight. They dislike beating around the bush, soft pedaling, or dishonesty.

What employees really don't like is being told *only* what they're doing wrong without being coached or trained on how to do it correctly, and never hearing positive comments when they perform well or improve.

In the situation just described, Ryan would have succeeded in *trust-building* if he had had two separate conversations with Lane:

- First, to tell her she needs to improve her communication skills, with specific examples explaining what he wants her to do differently. Then, he could suggest how she could improve—by attending training.
- Second, a separate conversation on a different day, to recognize her for the quality of her writing and build on her strength by naming specific examples of her writing that he valued.

Call 'em as you see 'em. But don't do both in the same conversation. Separating the conversations allows the listener to fully focus on each one and have adequate time to absorb and understand both, without cross-contamination or confusion about your intended messages. And your trust won't be "busted."

It's common that employees have areas of good performance and areas they need to improve. When you communicate honestly, separately, and specifically about each, people believe what you say in both cases—the good news and the "bad" news. This builds trust.

Tell the Truth and Call 'Em As You See 'Em—Separately	
 **Wrong Way**	"You do a good job overall and I want to give you this training opportunity." (Hidden agenda: "The real reason for the training is that you need to improve.")
 **Right Way**	"Lane, I want you to improve the way you communicate with your coworkers when you need their help, for example, when they're busy and on a deadline. Here's a seminar I think will help you do that." And at a different time: "Lane, your written instructions for the new process for customer X are clear and concise. Just what I wanted!"

Engagement WD-40 Tip #7

When you call 'em as you see 'em, you'll be respected. Your employees will say, "When I do it wrong, she tells me. When I do it right, she tells me. That's fair."

Use Engagement WD-40:

It keeps everything moving freely!

C. Do What You Say You Will Do

A furniture manufacturer received customer complaints about chairs with nicks in the finish. Management decided to kick off a "Quality First" program. They prepared for weeks. They hung a large banner in the plant, "We will ship no product unless it's perfect." They handed out coffee mugs, T-shirts, and hats emblazoned with "Quality First" at a huge "all-hands" kickoff meeting led by the company's CEO. "If you see a flaw on one of our chairs," he said, "I empower you to take it out of the production line and set it aside, over by the wall to be reworked. We will not ship imperfect furniture."

Employees were enthusiastic about "Quality First" and began inspecting the chairs carefully before they sent them to be packed and shipped. One by one, nicked chairs began to appear by the designated wall. As the hours passed, the supervisor saw that they would fall short of their production schedule for the day. He went over to the wall to take a closer look at the flawed chairs. Employees noticed the worried look on his face, which became more intense as the end of the shift drew nearer. Thirty minutes before quitting time, he rubbed a little polish on the nicks and put them back in line to be packed and shipped. He met his production quota and went home with a sigh of relief.

Of course, the employees saw this and realized that meeting the day's production schedule was more important than the new "Quality First" program. They even came up with a name for the wall where they had placed the flawed chairs: "the healing wall." They joked, "That wall is magic. If you have a defective chair, all you have to do is put it beside that wall for a few hours, and it gets healed."

Everything went back to normal and the employees stopped looking for flaws. The mistake was that management's *words* said one thing but their *actions* said the opposite. All the effort and money they spent on their "Quality First" program was not only wasted, but it was a "trust-buster." Employees no longer trusted that managers would do what they said they would do. "Quality First" became another "program of the month" that they knew would fade away like all the others. The next time managers want to introduce something new, people will just roll their eyes and wait for it to pass.

Experiences like this make it more difficult the next time you want to do something new. You'd be better off *doing nothing* than announcing a program and failing to carry through. Starting programs and letting them die puts you further into the trust "hole." You'll have to work harder to get out. (Sorry for the bad news, but we're just "calling 'em as we see 'em.")

Actions always speak louder than words to employees. I'll bet you've heard these comments:

> "I gave that suggestion to my supervisor, but never heard anything more about it. It just went into a black hole. So don't bother making suggestions." "I put in a request for my machine to be fixed and Samantha said she'd handle it, but three days have passed, nothing's been done, and I haven't heard a word."

If employees have experienced disappointments like those described here, there's lots of room for improving trust. The perception of trust by employees includes actions to keep promises. Keep a notepad with you at all times to jot down items you need to follow up on as you walk the Gemba workplace and hear from your employees. Don't trust your memory; you have far too many things coming at you during a typical day.

It's important to let employees know within 48 hours if their requests can be fulfilled, or if there's a reason why they cannot. *It's fine to say no*. Just say *something*. Leave no "unfinished business" with employees and coworkers to keep your relationships "caught up" and clear for the next challenge that comes along.

It's better to say "no" than to promise something and then let it slide.

*Pinch Point Warning #6: The danger of asking employees for suggestions is that you will soon be overloaded with more than you can handle. Create a standard procedure for others to act on suggestions without waiting for you.**

*For more on this, see *Design for Operational Excellence* by Kevin Duggan.

Do What You Say You Will Do	
 **Wrong Way**	"We couldn't do what Mac suggested, so I just dropped it."
 **Right Way**	"Mac, I want you to take your idea to the project team. Let me know what they decide. I appreciate you coming up with these new ideas for us."

D. Never Make Negative Statements about Other Employees. Tell Them to Their Faces What You Want Them to Improve

Janis's story

> *I had a boss who frequently complained to me about other employees who were my peers. As I sat in his office discussing a project, he would often make negative comments about others. This made me wonder what this boss might be saying to my coworkers about me when I wasn't around. My trust was busted.*

Pinch Point Warning #7: Don't "bad-mouth" anyone to others. If you need to correct an employee, speak to that person directly and in private. Tell her the truth about what she's doing wrong and coach her about how to improve.

Never Make Negative Statements About One Employee to Other Employees	
 **Wrong Way**	To others: "Phyllis is just not pulling her weight."
 **Right Way**	To Phyllis: "Phyllis, I expect you to complete all the items on the checklist today. Let's review your work at three-thirty."

On the brighter side, Mike's story

The first time I met Orelia Rogers, vice president of a logistics company, she asked two colleagues and me to help her implement a new process that would improve service to our customers. Two of Orelia's initial comments "hooked" me to be on her team: she said positive things about other people. "I'll ask Joe to help us," she said. "He's resourceful at finding shortcuts that work without sacrificing quality. And Carrie. She gets things done quickly." I had planned to leave work early that day, but I stayed later to start working on the team's project because I was enthusiastic about being on Orelia's team of talented people. Orelia was a trust builder.

Like Orelia, be generous with your positive talk about your employees when it's deserved. Remember, if people hear you making positive comments about their peers, they'll trust you to make positive comments about them. You can be a trust builder or a trustbuster with just a few words. Choose your words carefully.

E. Give Credit Where It's Earned

Shannon had an idea for a way to improve her department's response time to internal customers, which she knew had been a problem for the organization. She explained it to Frank, her supervisor, who answered, "I don't have time to make any changes right now. Maybe later." In a meeting the next day, a colleague brought up the problem of long response times, and Frank, feeling on the spot, said, "I have an idea I'm working on to make responses faster. I should have it ready by next week." Then Frank went back to Shannon and said, "Go ahead and do it. Track your response time compared with last week's and give me the data Monday morning."

Shannon did it. The response time with her new method was 50% faster. Frank took Shannon's data to his meeting and announced that his idea had worked and would solve the problem. A colleague complimented Frank and asked how his department had done it. Frank said, "I'd been working on this for a while. The timing was right to tell my team to go ahead with the new process."

A few days later, one of the people at the meeting casually mentioned it to Shannon: "How do you like Frank's new process for answering internal customer requests?" Shannon said, "I like it a lot. I should; it was my idea." The person said, "That's funny. Frank told us in the staff meeting it was an idea he'd been working on for a while. He didn't mention your name."

After several similar incidents happened, Shannon asked for a transfer to another department. When Frank asked her why, Shannon said, "I don't think I would ever have a chance for advancing my career in your department." Frank apparently didn't know that by giving credit and recognition to his employee, he himself would also have looked good. By stealing the credit, he lost Shannon's trust *and* lost a good idea-person.

Think about successful sports coaches. They don't claim to have caught the pass or scored the basket. They look good because they coached the players who did.

Give Credit Where It's Earned	
 **Wrong Way**	"Yes, that was my idea."
 **Right Way**	"Jon invented a way to overcome several obstacles so the project was completed ahead of time."

Also, build a positive culture by recognizing individuals for their "easy-to-take-for-granted" everyday productive behaviors. Nothing formal or fancy—quick, personal acknowledgments mean more than you might think! And—share the compliments with *your* boss. Give credit where it's earned.

Engagement WD-40 Tip #8

Say positive things to your employees about their coworkers.

Use Engagement WD-40

It keeps everything moving freely!

QUIZ (answers on next page)	
1.	Your actions as a leader can be trust-____________ or trust-____________.
2.	As a leader giving feedback to your employees, call 'em as you _______ ____.
3.	It's better to say _____ than to promise something and let it slide.

ANSWERS TO QUIZ	
1.	builders . . . busters
2.	see 'em
3.	no

Summary Checklist

- As a leader, take actions that are trust builders, not trust-busters.
- Tell the truth, even if it's difficult for both people in the conversation.
- Do what you say you will do. Take notes to help you remember what you've committed to do.
- Never make negative statements about other employees. Tell them to their faces what you want them to improve.
- Give credit where it's earned.

Chapter 13

How to Measure Your Success

Key Points

A. Measure: Individuals doing things
B. Measure: Teams explaining their projects
C. Measure your role: Leader Standard Work to engage, involve, and motivate

When Janis told a company president she was cowriting a book titled *How to Engage, Involve, and Motivate Employees*, he commented, “Oh, yes, we have employee engagement. We do a survey every other year.” As a reader of this book, you would now be able to tell him the difference between survey scores and actual engagement—whether his employees are *doing* things that make measurable improvement—not just talk or a checked box on a survey:

Doing  vs. checking the “engaged” box ✓

Which do you want?

We measure engagement by actions—individual actions and team actions that measurably contribute to our results.

A. Measure: Individuals Doing Things

If you think about all the people you work with, you'll notice *by their actions* that some are more engaged, involved, and motivated than others. Dr. Aubrey Daniels, author of *Bringing Out the Best in People*, identified five behaviors in employees that indicate engagement:

1. They willingly lend a hand to coworkers, even when they aren't asked.
2. They aren't clock-watchers; they often show up early or stay late* to complete the work.
3. They offer ideas and solutions for improvements.
4. They acknowledge others' accomplishments and are pleased with their success.
5. They quickly volunteer to lead or assist in implementing initiatives outside their immediate work area.

These actions are the "blocking and tackling" basics of engagement. When you see or hear about an employee doing these five things, be sure to let him know you noticed. You'll be giving positive recognition for his behaviors of engagement, and you'll get more of them!

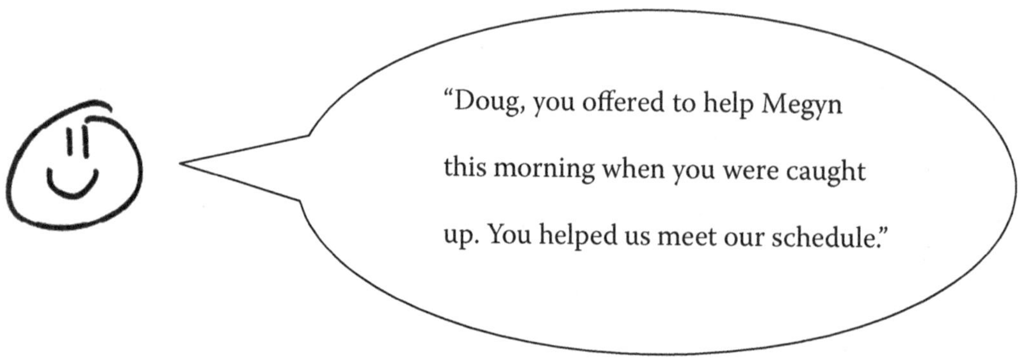

B. Measure: Teams Explaining Their Projects

If your team members can point to projects they have completed and describe the actions they took to get there, you have success. As we asked in Chapter 1, suppose a visitor came to your department and asked, "Are

* Staying late may or may not fit with overtime pay policies for some employees.

your employees engaged?" Could you take her to your department and ask any employee to talk the visitor through an improvement project and its measurable results? If so, congratulations! You have engaged, involved, and motivated employees.

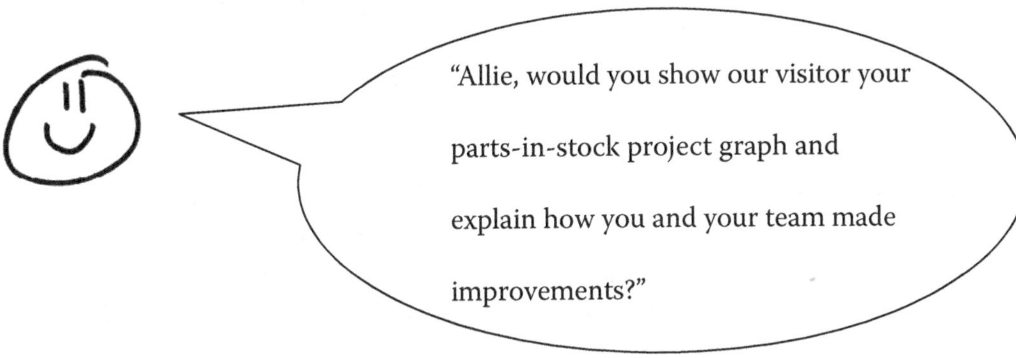

Here's an example of a graph your employees will be able to explain if they are engaged (the gray bars show actual improvement):

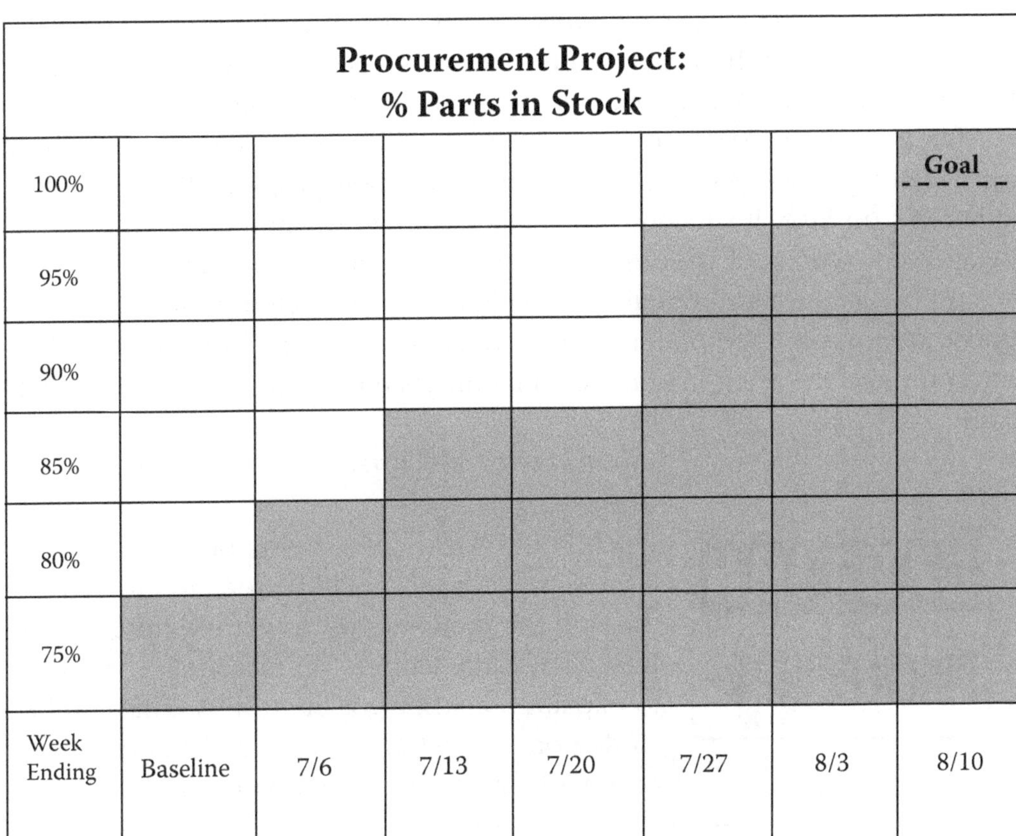

Janis's story

A project engineer led a kaizen event that concluded with the kaizen team moving some equipment to change the work flow. The next morning, the equipment had all been moved back to its original place. No one had communicated with the night shift, so they did what made sense to them. I asked the engineer what he did next. "I went on to the next kaizen event. I have goals for 18 kaizen events a year. We have to report to corporate, so I had no time to go back to last week's team."

What a waste! The process stayed the same after all that work.

Engagement success cannot be measured by the number of teams, the number of kaizen events, scores on an engagement survey, or even the number of projects. If your employees can't explain measurable improvement projects they've implemented, circle back to Chapters 4 through 8. Your employees are ready when you are!

We want "consciously competent" team members. That means they got the result and they can explain *how* they got the result. In this way, other teams can learn how to do the same thing.

Keep a list of the employees who are working on each project. At least twice a week, go to the Gemba (the office or shop floor where the actual work is done) and ask employees to tell you about their projects in process.

After a week or two, take your boss with you (after coaching her to listen and to tell the employees what she likes about their projects). It's accountability. It's positive. It's recognition. This recognition will increase the engagement actions of your employees. Your job just got easier.

And by taking your boss along, you just gave yourself a mini-performance review—a good one! Like a major league scout looking at your players, your boss is seeing in *your* team members the results of *your* coaching skills.

Your job just got easier.

Pinch Point Warning #8: If you only count the number of projects, you'll be tempted to "go through the motions" just to get the numbers up. Instead, ask the teams with measurable results to explain *how* they got the results. This can be shown on a storyboard, A-3, our 5-Step Model, or any other problem-solving model.

C. Measure Your Role: Leader Standard Work to Engage, Involve, and Motivate

Take the actions shown on the Leader Standard Work checklist during your Gemba walks,* Toolbox† Meetings, and any time you have contact with employees. Note the name of the person with whom you took the actions. This is feedback to yourself on how frequently you're engaging, involving, and motivating all your employees.

Overall Checklist for Leader Standard Work to Engage, Involve, and Motivate Employees through Projects Leader's Name: ____________							
Leader/Supervisor Actions		Initials of Person(s)with Whom I Took these Actions					
		M	T	W	T	F	S
1.	Asked for ideas for specific improvements						
2.	Invited people to join a project team						
3.	Coached, set goals, gave feedback						
4.	Gave positive recognition for productive behaviors I saw, and positive solutions I heard						
5.	Trained someone how to do tasks, delegated to develop skills						
6.	Called individual(s) by name						

QUIZ (answers on next page)	
1.	"Consciously competent" employees got results and can __________ how they got the results.
2.	Gemba walks are when you go into the work area to ____ for __________ how the project is going.

* Gemba walks: Going into the work area to do personal observations of the work—where the work is happening. The original Japanese term is "Gemba Gembutsu," which means "go to where the work is done and see for yourself."

† Toolbox Meetings: Brief, informal stand-up meetings with a supervisor or team leader and her employees, often to talk about safety, but can be used for other topics.

ANSWERS TO QUIZ	
1.	explain
2.	see . . . yourself

Summary Checklist

- Get individuals actively doing things.
- Ask team members to explain their projects.
- Use the checklist of Leader Standard Work to engage, involve, and motivate.

Chapter 14

When Correcting Is Needed: Deal with Negatives and Move On

Key Points

A. **Deal with negative issues individually (not in groups), specifically (no generalities), and quickly (no procrastinating). Then move on.**
B. **Coach for correct behaviors and give recognition when the person improves.**

Sometimes you will have an employee who doesn't follow the rules or doesn't perform. You may be tempted to ignore this. But just as machine problems get worse when you ignore them, behaviors often do too. Best to deal with the problem while it's still a small problem. Letting it go is bad for engagement, bad for teamwork, bad for projects, bad for morale, and bad for your business.

A. Deal with Negative Issues Individually (Not in Groups), Specifically (No Generalities), and Quickly (No Procrastinating). Then, Move On

Here's what happens when you ignore a problem or procrastinate dealing with it:

Cathy arrived late two or three days a week. She always had excuses. "I overslept." "My dog ran off and I had to go find him." "My son missed the school bus and I had to drive him to school."

Other team members noticed that Cathy had gotten away with arriving late week after week. No one wanted to confront her because she was good at her job. Other people began seeing that they could get away with arriving late and the problem became much larger. Customer orders weren't completed on time. Complaints rolled in.

Warnings were given at team meetings. Finally, everyone was told they had to start scanning their badges on a time clock. What if Cathy's supervisor had handled this problem with Cathy immediately? Others would not have been required to start "scanning in," and the company's reputation with customers wouldn't have suffered.

Too often, we see a whole group of employees punished for one person's behavior. Individual, face-to-face correcting is never easy, but it almost always prevents bigger problems. We've emphasized motivating with positive recognition in this book, but that does not mean that you ignore poor performance, troublemaking actions, or deliberate unsafe acts. When an employee refuses to follow policies or does not attempt to improve her performance, give her specific instructions on how to improve. Tell her what will happen for failure to comply and firm timelines.

As a leader, if you fail to deal quickly and firmly with problems, you'll get more of them. You will actually be creating a negative culture—negative for all the other employees who see what's happening but have to pick up the slack for a nonperforming member of the team. Worse, it implies that this behavior is OK. And some will even pick up the message that they need not obey rules either.

> *As a leader, if you fail to deal quickly and firmly with problems, you'll get more of them.*

B. Coach for Correct Behaviors and Give Recognition When the Person Improves

After you firmly set expectations for someone who's performing incorrectly or insufficiently, give him a task, a small first step he can take to begin to "turn his performance around" within 24 hours. This puts the focus on actions for improvement.

Deal Individually, Specifically, and Quickly with Problems	
 **Wrong Way**	"Just leave it alone. He might get better. If it continues, I'll deal with him later."
 **Right Way**	"Jon, when you come in late, others have to do your work. I want you here on time every day. If you're late again, you'll have two points added to the eight you have on your tardiness record. Ten will put you on probation. I've made this graph to post your arrival time each day. Bring it to me when you arrive—on time—tomorrow, and we'll post it together."

Make a point to "go to the Gemba" (go where the work is done) and observe whether he completes these actions. If he does, immediately make a specific positive comment to him privately about what you observed. For instance, "I see you're here on time, Jon." Nothing flowery or loud.

This immediate feedback communicates to him

1. That you expect him to perform and will watch and hold him accountable
2. That *he* is in control of getting himself "out of the hole" and on track to acceptable performance if he continues to take the actions you expect

Your immediate positive comments can become positive motivators as long as he *earns* them. Give him another goal, observe, and coach if needed, but give a small positive reinforcing comment if he earns it. At the end of the week, say, "On time for five days, Jon. Good!"

In other words, use the negative consequences (warnings, probation) when someone is headed in the wrong direction. This gets their attention to help him head in the right direction.

Most people will see this as fair: "He told me when I was wrong and he told me when I was right. OK, that's fair."

Be quick to give the positive comment when it is *earned*. Not before it's earned, and not as a bribe.* For instance, don't say, "I'll go ahead and remove these absenteeism points because now that we've talked, I know you're committed to being at work every day." (Commitment is not action. Commitment is talk.)

Make a point to observe whether he completes the correct action. If he does, immediately make a specific positive comment, privately.

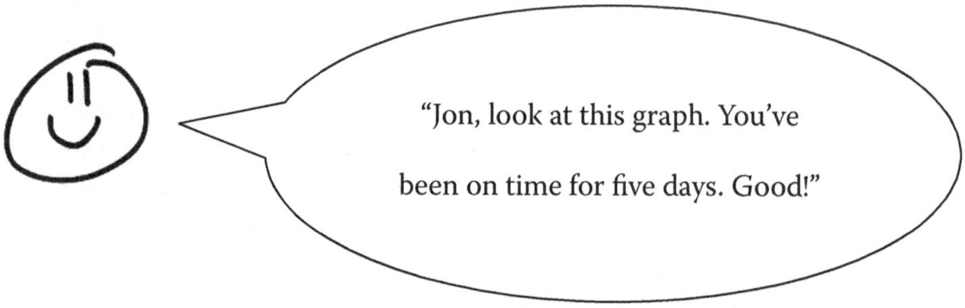

Don't worry, I'm not suggesting that you "babysit" a person's behaviors every day forever with these small goals and your immediate observations. After he's met the goals you've set for him, begin to extend the times to two days, three days, and a week. Give frequent positive recognition during the first week when he completes the actions to your satisfaction, then "thin out" the schedule of goals, observations, and recognition to once or twice

* Bribe: Giving the positive thing before it is earned. Rarely works to get the correct behavior. Don't do it.

per week. Soon, he will blend in with your other good-performing employees. You'll be frequently reinforcing him *along with the others* for their productive behaviors anyway. Right?

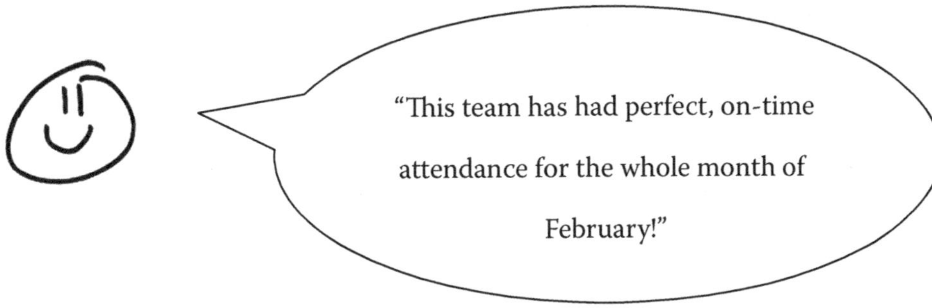

Jon is now *part of the team* that has earned your recognition.

Correcting with the Help of a Checklist

Here's an example of a graph you and your employees can use to set specific expectations, set goals, and measure progress, That serves as a reminder for you to give recognition when it's earned.

Ask the employee to keep the data by putting her own checks in the boxes when she has completed the correct procedure (the best way to engage and involve her). Your recognition will be the motivator for her to continue.

Checklist of Correct Procedures Used by ______________ (name)					
5				✓	✓
4			✓		
3		✓			
2	✓				
1					
	Monday	Tuesday	Wednesday	Thursday	Friday

Engagement WD-40 Tip #9

Deal with negatives individually, specifically, and quickly.

Then move on.

Use Engagement WD-40:

It keeps everything moving freely!

QUIZ (answers on next page)	
1.	Deal with negative issues _____________ (not in groups), _____________ (no generalities), and _____________ (no procrastinating). Then, move on.
2.	Coach for correct behaviors and give recognition when it's ___________.

ANSWERS TO QUIZ	
1.	individually . . . specifically . . . quickly
2.	earned

Summary Checklist

- Deal with negative issues individually (not in groups), specifically (no generalities), and quickly (no procrastinating). Then, move on.
- Coach for correct behaviors and give recognition when the person improves.

Chapter 15

FMMs (Frequently Made Mistakes): Troubleshooting and Preventing Them

Key Points

A. **Don't start an "engagement program" for scores on a survey. Don't start an "engagement program" if you aren't prepared to follow up on the employee ideas you receive.**
B. **Deal with negative talk and behaviors by choosing where your attention goes. Give no attention to negative talk. Give your attention to productive talk.**
C. **Learn from past mistakes.**

Many obstacles to successful engagement, involvement, and motivation can be prevented *before* they become obstacles. The tips in this chapter will help you prevent those obstacles or overcome them if they already exist.

A. Don't Start an "Engagement Program" for Scores on a Survey. Don't Start an "Engagement Program" if You Aren't Prepared to Follow Up on the Employee Ideas You Receive

And don't call it an engagement program. Don't call it anything. Just start engaging. Engagement is a tool to improve business results. Using a tool for the sake of using a tool is useless. Imagine giving carpenters a "hammering survey." Hammering what? To build what?

The Reason to Engage and Involve Employees	
 **Wrong Way**	"Let's get some employees in our department together and brainstorm. We can report it as a team meeting, and they'll give us better scores on the next engagement survey."
 **Right Way**	"I need your help to improve the on-time delivery for our largest customer"

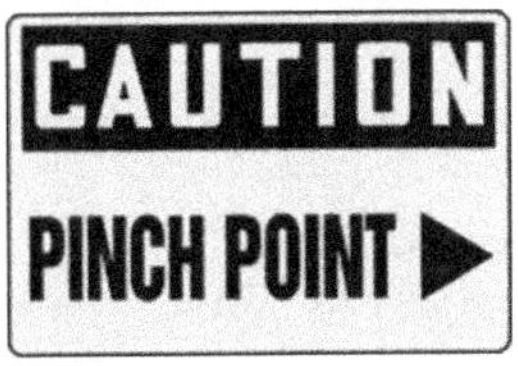

Pinch Point Warning #9: You will do more harm than good if you ask for ideas but have no plan for acting on them *within one week*. First, develop a process for reviewing ideas, giving feedback, and taking action. Be ready to form a project team to test the improvement ideas right away.

Many announced "programs" have done more harm than good. When managers decide to implement a new program, they're often tempted to make a big to-do of it with kickoff meetings, banners (remember "Quality First" at the chair manufacturing plant?), T-shirts, and hats. Expectations are set high for all involved to behave according to the program guidelines. So when a leader fails to execute the program perfectly, employees may become disillusioned and lose trust that leaders are serious.

So don't give it a name. Don't talk about it. Don't have a kickoff. Save the T-shirts and pizza for a celebration of the success of an improvement project *after* the measurable improvement is made, not before.

Just start an improvement project. People will respond to your genuine interest in their ideas. Get interested in *their ideas*. Don't get interested in a "program."

Engagement WD-40 Tip #10

Don't call it an engagement program.

Don't call it anything. Don't announce it.

Just do it! Test an idea.

Use Engagement WD-40:

It keeps everything moving freely!

How to Get Engagement and Involvement	
 **Wrong Way**	"We're kicking off a new engagement program."
 **Right Way**	"Molly, you have lots of experience with this problem. Would you give me your ideas on ways we can solve it?"

B. Deal with Negative Talk and Behaviors by Choosing Where Your Attention Goes. Give No Attention to Negative Talk. Give Your Attention to Productive Talk

Mike's Story:

An employee for a trucking company said, "I used to come to work thinking of ways I could (pardon the language) screw the company over. Now, I come to work thinking of ways I can help the company." What caused the change? Months earlier, his supervisor had begun looking for behaviors that employees were doing right—and their ideas—and commenting positively. This was much different from only mentioning the things they were doing wrong. This supervisor had built trust with this employee by focusing on behaviors the employee had done well.

You may find that some employees resist becoming engaged and involved, and seem to be coming to work simply to get a paycheck. They may be holding grudges from perceived or real mistreatment or from not having their ideas listened to in the past. Don't spend a lot of time and energy dwelling on the past. You may gain that person's trust and engagement by asking him about his reluctance in private (never in a group meeting). Listen. Acknowledge his feelings. Say, "I understand that you feel negatively about this." But don't try to convince him that he shouldn't feel that way.

Many people (not all) will "let go" of negative feelings when they truly feel heard. Later, you can ask for his ideas on a specific issue, listen carefully to his ideas if he's ready to offer them, and decide how to test one of his ideas. Look for behaviors he's doing that are positive and productive and name them specifically. It may take several times for him to accept your positive recognition without sarcasm (!!). Together, you and that person are taking the first step toward rebuilding trust.

Overcoming Negative Experiences or Trust Issues	
 **Wrong Way**	"Why aren't you cooperating on this project?"
 **Right Way**	"I know you had an idea that was ignored last year. Would you tell me that idea again?"

Warning: you can't change everyone. Use the Pareto Principle (the 80/20 rule) to determine how you spend your valuable time. Don't spend 80% of your time with the 20% of "negative people" challenges. If you do, your "negative people" challenges will increase, while the productive employees you're ignoring will have no motivation to maintain their good performance. Spend 80% of your time with the 80% of your team members who are productive.

Pinch Point Warning #10:
Don't spend more of your time trying to persuade the naysayer than you spend with the people who are engaged and involved. This sends the message that the best way to get attention is to be negative.

C. Learn from Past Mistakes

In 1982, seven people died after taking Tylenol that had been tampered with and put back on store shelves. Johnson & Johnson, the maker, moved quickly to recall the entire product from all stores. People stopped buying Tylenol, of course. Soon Johnson & Johnson announced new packaging, which customers could clearly see was double sealed for safety, and put Tylenol back in stores. They didn't just advertise how safe Tylenol would be. Customers saw their *actions*. Today, it's a best-selling pain medicine.

To rebuild trust, actions speak louder than words.

If your employees (and you) have had a negative experience or a bumpy ride with employee engagement, at least you're learning. This puts you several steps on your way to a positive experience because you've learned *what not to do*.

We look at obstacles or bumps as "success trials," because every experience helps us learn how to do better next time. Obstacles help us learn.

Or as Garry Ridge, CEO of WD-40 Company writes in his book (with Ken Blanchard) *Helping People Win at Work*, "At WD-40 Company, when things go wrong, we don't call them 'mistakes'; we call them 'Learning Moments.'"

Write down your learning experiences to share with your coworkers as you plan to take more steps toward success (or better yet, ask your employees for their input to make this list):

Lessons Learned from Our Projects		
What We Did	What Went Wrong	What We Learned

Increasing Successes

You've probably had some good results as you involved your employees. Let's learn from your success. With your employees, think of what you've done that has worked, and make notes:

Lessons Learned from Successes in Our Projects		
What We Did	What Went Well	What We Learned

QUIZ (answers on next page)	
1.	Don't give too much attention to ____________ talk. Give most of your attention to ____________ talk.
2.	You can do more harm than good if you ask for ideas but have no plan for acting on them within _____ week.
3.	Don't call it an engagement program. Don't call it anything. Don't announce it. Just ___ ___!

ANSWERS TO QUIZ	
1.	negative . . . positive
2.	one
3.	do it

Summary Checklist

- Don't call it an engagement program. Don't call it anything. Just start asking employees for ideas to improve your processes.
- Give no attention to negative talk. Give your attention to productive talk.
- Learn from past mistakes and put your learning to good use.

Chapter 16

Grow More Leaders

The success of a coach is the success of his or her team members.

Key Point

When you're building leaders, support their growth with goals, asking for their ideas, training, delegating, feedback, coaching, and recognition.

Why grow more leaders? Leaders are self-starters. When you grow more self-starters, your job gets easier. Self-starters come to you with project ideas, so you don't always have to be the person to initiate the ideas. Self-starters are, by definition, engaged, and they can help you engage others. Your job gets easier.

How Someone Grew Me as a Leader

Janis's story

Mike Georgion

The best mentor of my career, Mike Georgion at Milliken & Company, challenged me to develop a Performance Leadership training course for our division's plant managers (this is the ***Project PULL*** *that you've learned about in this book). Previously, I had only worked with people at my plant, and I told Mike that I didn't know if I could create material for these high-level managers. Mike just nodded and gave me a list of what he considered to be the plant managers' needs* *for developing skills (****Mike was asking for specific ideas****, which you've learned about) and asked if I'd think about it for a week before saying no. He suggested I write down any ideas I had for the new course (****Mike was setting a GOAL****—sound familiar?) and meet with him in a week. I had my doubts but agreed.*

For the next week, it was all I could think about (as you know, ***projects PULL people!****). Mike's list of needs plus my experience and observations set me off on a bumper crop of ideas. I could hardly write them down as fast as they came. By the time our next meeting date arrived, I had organized my ideas into a detailed outline and was excited about the project.*

*Mike reviewed my ideas, named what he liked (****giving me feedback****), asked questions (****using the Socratic Method****), and approved my outline (****giving me recognition****).*

*He said, "Let's offer your first module as a pilot class (****testing my idea****). Afterward, I'll ask the participants if they will attend another module. If the majority say yes, that will tell us that these internal customers will 'buy' more of what we're 'selling,' and we'll schedule more modules." (****With this plan, Mike was using data and internal customer PULL.****) They "bought," and the course was expanded.*

*Mike suggested that I build in improvement projects as part of the course, so we'd be able to measure the success of the course by the participants' project results (****using measurable project data****). The data showed improved results, and the course was later extended to other divisions.*

My skills increased and my confidence soared. Mike had grown me into a leader. This new level of experience and confidence gave me the basis to grow and help others grow. Soon, I was promoted and given the job to lead other people in my field and to help them to succeed.

After that experience, I became a consultant, worked with dozens of organizations all over the United States, published five business books, founded a company, and trained other people to conduct the training I created. I was engaged, involved, and motivated. And it all started with Mike Georgion's Project PULL: asking for my ideas, setting goals, and giving me coaching, feedback, and recognition.

You can see why I believe so strongly in this process. And you can see from my example that this method works with any type of job, not just manufacturing.

As employees become more engaged and involved, they are learning new skills and seeing the bigger picture of your business. Support their growth by giving more responsibility to those who are interested.

Sometimes, leaders have to give employees a little encouragement to try something new. If the leader states the goal specifically and asks the employee for his or her ideas, the employee will often become energized and motivated to take on more responsibility. Mike's specific request and his confidence in me formed the perfect formula to grow another leader! I will always be grateful to Mike Georgion.

Grow More Leaders

1. Find out what people are interested in doing.
2. Ask for their ideas on a specific task.
3. Coach people with the assumption that they'll succeed.
4. Train them, set a goal, then step aside. Schedule feedback.
5. Don't just point out mistakes; coach for improvement.
6. Give attention to the good performance we usually take for granted.

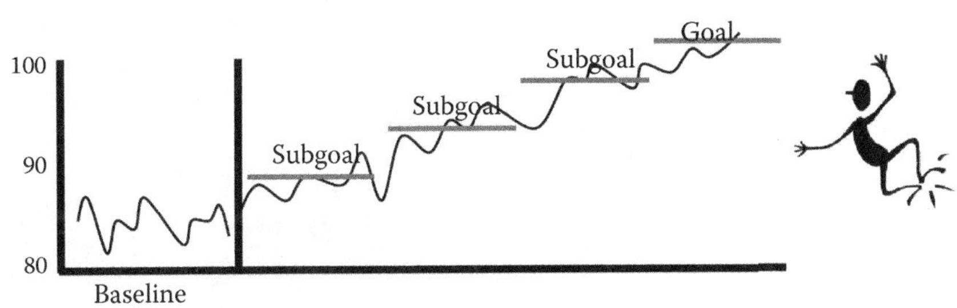

QUIZ (answers on next page)	
1.	Why grow more leaders? Because leaders are self-____________.
2.	Sometimes leaders have to give employees a little ______________ to get them to try something new.

ANSWERS TO QUIZ	
1.	starters
2.	encouragement

Summary Checklist

- When you're building leaders, support their growth with goals, asking for their ideas, training, delegating, feedback, coaching, and recognition.

Appendix I: Launch Guide* to Engage, Involve, and Motivate Employees

1. Look for improvement projects to PULL people
   a. With your employee(s), go to the Gemba (workplace) and walk your production process.
   b. Look for flow blockage/delay.
   c. Ask, "What would make the work flow easier or faster?"
   d. Ask your customers and supervisor what they would like improved.
2. Let the project determine how many people to engage
   a. Start with one person on one task.
   b. As you see the need for more tasks or additional skills, add people.
3. Ask for ideas on projects and specific improvements
   a. Ask employee(s) for help on a specific project or problem.
   b. Brainstorm for ideas with your group or individual employee.
   c. Write down ALL ideas.
   d. Accept all ideas gratefully, even before determining if they can be used.
   e. Pick one to three ideas to test.
   f. Level the ideas (Level 1, 2, or 3) so actions can be taken immediately.
   g. Log the action items, volunteers, and target dates.
4. Set time targets to test ideas
   a. With your employees' input set a goal and subgoals for testing ideas.

---

* With thanks to David Visco for this Launch Guide design from his book *5S Made Easy* (Productivity Press, 2015).

   b. Coach employees to help them perform action steps to meet the goals for the test.
   c. Recognize employees for their actions completed.
5. Motivate actions with positive recognition
   a. Notice productive actions: Use EPT (**E**ye contact, **P**oint to the action, **T**humbs up) or quick positive comments (verbal underlining "Trebek-style").
   b. Hold small "Proud Time" conversations or team celebrations to name the behaviors that helped you succeed.
6. Coach with feedback: verbal, data, and graphs
   a. Tell and show employees daily and weekly how they are progressing on the project.
   b. Coach employees to post their own graphs and checklists to track their progress.
   c. Post your progress on results (compared to the date you began the project).
7. Complete, then repeat
   a. Celebrate your success, then look for another improvement project.
   b. Repeat so that these steps of engagement, involvement, and motivation become habits (your culture) for the leader and the employees. ***That's continuous improvement!***

Appendix II: Pinch Point Warnings: The Collection

Here are all the Pinch Points covered in the book—here in one place for you to review and avoid!

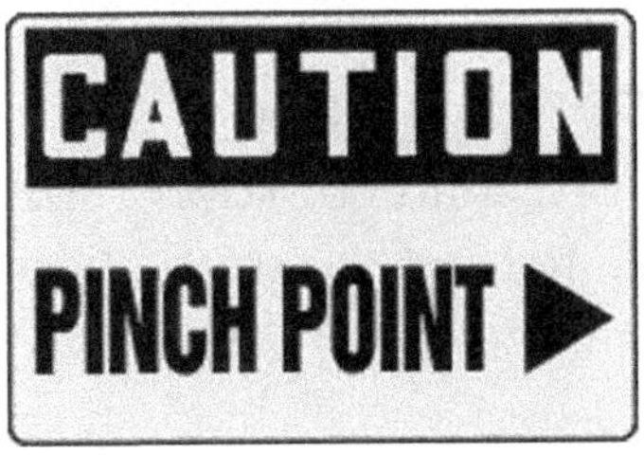

Pinch Point Warning #1: Don't make the mistake of focusing only on survey results. Even the most uninvolved employee can check the "I'm engaged" box on a survey. Instead, ask people for ideas on improvements *they* can make. Then recruit a team to test the idea.

Pinch Point Warning #2: You could "pinch" off your coworkers' flow of ideas with your negative comments. Then they'll stop giving you ideas. Instead, choose ideas to test.

Pinch Point Warning #3: When you give positive recognition, let it stand alone. Don't follow it by talking about more work you want the person to do, or a higher goal. For example, "Darren, you've reached your goal of 80% production. But your quality still needs improvement." Give your positive recognition and STOP. This will give your positive recognition time to sink in and have maximum effect. Handle new goals or needs for improvement at a *different time*.

Pinch Point Warning #4: Keep your graphs up to date or take them down. Out-of-date graphs become wallpaper and teach team members to *ignore* what you post on performance boards.

Pinch Point Warning #5: Putting people on the team without a job to do is asking for trouble. They will make a job for themselves—criticizing, whining, or blocking.

Pinch Point Warning #6: The danger of asking for employee suggestions and requests is that you will soon be overloaded with more than you can handle. Create a standard procedure for others to act on suggestions without waiting for you.

Pinch Point Warning #7: Don't "bad-mouth" anyone to others. If you need to correct an employee, speak to that person directly and in private. Tell her the truth about what she's doing wrong and coach her about how to improve.

Pinch Point Warning #8: If you only count the number of projects, you'll be tempted to "go through the motions" just to get the numbers up. Instead, ask the teams with measurable results to explain *how* they got the results. This can be shown on a storyboard, A-3, our 5-Step Model, or any other problem-solving model.

Pinch Point Warning #9: You will do more harm than good if you ask for ideas but have no plan for acting on them *within one week*. First, develop a process for reviewing ideas, giving feedback, and taking action. Be ready to form a project team to test the improvement ideas right away.

Pinch Point Warning #10: Don't spend more of your time trying to persuade the naysayer than you spend with the people who are engaged and involved. This sends the message that the best way to get attention is to be negative.

Appendix III: Engagement WD-40 Tips: The Collection

Use Engagement WD-40 to Keep Everything Moving Freely

Here are all the Engagement WD-40 Tips in the book. Come here and review them often!

Tip #1: Ask employees to go see how the work could be made easier. This is PULL and avoids the PUSH of "telling." Projects PULL people.

Tip #2: Specificity Succeeds. *Specificity* succeeds when we ask others for their ideas by giving them something concrete to respond to.

Tip #3: Use your employees' and coworkers' names often. This reaffirms that your focus is on them and shows respect. It gets their attention and paves the way for engagement.

Tip #4: Use EPT for quick recognition in the Gemba (workplace)

Eye contact

Point to the work

Thumbs up

Tip #5: Coach employees in how to use graphs and checklists to track their own progress.

Tip #6: Build a team one person at a time. How? Invite them.

Tip #7: When you call 'em as you see 'em, you'll be respected. Your employees will say, "When I do it wrong, she tells me. When I do it right, she tells me. That's fair."

Tip #8: Say positive things to your employees about their coworkers.

Tip #9: Deal with negatives individually, specifically, and quickly. Then, move on.

Tip #10: Don't call it an engagement program. Don't call it anything. Don't announce it. Just do it! Test an idea.

Appendix IV: Find a Project and Pick the Team

GEMBA GEMBUTSU
(Japanese phrase meaning "go to the workplace and see for yourself.")

1. SEE THE DEFECT

Find ways to prevent the defect.

2. SEE THE STRAIN or MURI (the Japanese word for too much work or too difficult)

Find ways to balance the workload and/or make work easier.

3. SEE THE WASTE or MUDA* (wasted motion or process steps)

Find ways to reduce the seven wastes of lean.*

* For an explanation of the seven wastes, see Sustain Your Gains by Michael McCarthy, available at the5sstore.com.

CHECKLIST OF WHAT TO LOOK FOR IN THE WORKFLOW:

- What slows you down?
- What gets in your way?
- When do you have to do extra walking?
- When does something go wrong?
- Where are the bottlenecks?
- Where are there stacks of WIP (work in process) waiting to be processed?
- People reaching or stretching more than an arm's length for tools or material. People bending or squatting to do the work.
- People waiting for a machine to finish processing a part.
- People waiting for parts, tools, material, or WIP.
- People repairing or reworking a part that has already gone through the process.

When you **SEE** ANY OF THESE THINGS, YOU HAVE A POTENTIAL PROJECT AIMED TO

- Reduce it.
- Eliminate it.
- Cut out an extra step.
- Make it easier to do.
- Make it safer to do.
- Change the process to make a good part the first time.
- Reduce the amount of walking needed to do the task.
- Redistribute the workload among operators so that WIP (work in process) does not "pile up" at one workstation.
- Redistribute the workload (level loading) so that no one operator has to strain to keep up.
- Rearrange the workstation so that no strain (stretching, bending, or squatting) is necessary to do the task.

Where to begin? Go SEE where		
1.	Customers (internal or external) are complaining about something or asking for something	
2.	The boss has shown you our priorities	
3.	Mistakes are repeated in your department's work flow	
4.	The competition is beating us	
Walk the work flow with your team members and ask them		
5.	What problems or mistakes do you see most often?	
6.	What requests or complaints have we received from the downstream departments (our internal customers)?	
7.	What "workarounds" of the current process do you find yourself doing?	
8.	What can we do to make our work easier to do and flow more smoothly?	

Goal: Pick a project to start on. With your employee(s), prioritize your list. If "yes," make a check mark below.				
Project Idea List	Biggest Problem*	Helps Work Flow?	Helps Customers?	We Can Do It Ourselves?
Suggestion: Start with the one with the most checks.				

*Exception to biggest problem rule: If you and your employee(s) are new to group problem solving, then pick an easy problem that can be solved in one or two weeks.

Pick the Team! *Project:* ______			
Names of Individuals	Have Availability?	Have Needed Skill?	Have Needed Knowledge?

Appendix V: Brainstorming

Checklist for Successful Brainstorming

1. Brainstorming can be in the Gemba (workplace) as well as in a meeting room.
2. You can hold a mini-brainstorm at the point of need. Take a legal pad and walk to the actual part of the process that needs improving.
3. Write your brainstorming *topic* (what you need to improve or solve) at the top of a tabletop flip chart (or legal pad).
4. **Ask** for ideas: "How can we improve/solve this?"
5. Write down **all** ideas exactly as they are spoken (this is very important). No editing. **No judgments** or criticism allowed from anyone in the group. You may also ask people to write their ideas on the page as they speak them.
6. Ask participants to **pick** the ideas they want to test first. Circle the top 1–3 ideas picked. Don't strike through ideas in an effort to pare down the list before voting. Just pick those you think might work and plan ways to test them.
7. When ideas are mentioned that aren't directly related to this issue, write them on a separate sheet named "The Parking Lot." Save it and come back to it later when you're ready to focus on that issue.

Appendix VI: Which Level Is This Idea?

Here's a template to help you determine whether your idea is Level 1, 2, or 3:

Which Level Is This Idea?				
		Level 1 ***Go!***	**Level 2** ***Need to ask others***	**Level 3** ***Need to get more info***
1	Will downstream or upstream departments be affected if we make this change?	No	Another department or customer	Don't know
2	Do we need help from anyone outside our team or department?	Our team only	Another department or customer	Don't know
3	Would implementing this idea require other changes in our process or the process of another department?	No	If yes, recruit people from the customer's or other departments to join your team and help	Uncertain, need to research or test it
4	Will this idea's implementation change the "appearance," function, or ease of use of our finished product or service from the customer's point of view? *Example: When Amazon introduced the Kindle, they made pages that turned with a swipe of the finger exactly the way we do with paper pages in a book. Amazon preserved "ease of use" for reluctant-to-change customers. Result: The Kindle and Kindle books sell like hotcakes!*	No	Yes. Ask customers and/or sales/marketing people	Uncertain, need to research

When you've decided whether each idea is Level 1, 2, or 3, follow these steps:

Level 1 Ideas

1. Ask the individual who contributed this idea, "What are the steps to get started testing this idea?"
2. Write the steps on your team log.
3. Ask for volunteers to do each of these steps and write their names next to the steps. Encourage people *other than* the person who contributed the idea to volunteer. If the idea-person is always expected to do the work, he may stop offering ideas (wouldn't you?).
4. Ask each volunteer to write his or her own target date on the log.
5. Give positive recognition to those who volunteer for action items. Then later, give recognition to those who completed the actions.

Level 2 Ideas

1. List the other departments, employees, or customers who would be affected by the implementation of this Level 2 idea.
2. Ask for volunteers to invite those people to the next meeting, when the team members will explain the proposed idea. With the help of these other people, brainstorm
   a. How can we do this idea without adversely affecting your department?
   b. What changes would your department need to make?
   c. How can we work together to make these changes easier to make?
   d. Make a plan to communicate when you'll start using this idea, and when the decision will be made to use it as the new standard work process.
   e. Ask your guests if they will help you test this idea.
3. Modify your plan based on the input of these affected people.
4. Ask for volunteers to take the action items in that plan (add these to your team log), and write names and due dates on the log.
5. Follow up with those volunteers on the due dates. Recognize those who took actions.

6. On your team log, create a plan to check with the affected individuals and/or departments as the idea is implemented and for two to four weeks after the implementation to
   a. See if any adjustments are needed
   b. Verify that the idea is having the desired positive effects
   c. Give recognition to individuals from other departments who helped you

Level 3 Ideas

1. Determine what extra information is needed to make this idea a Level 1 or a Level 2.
2. Ask for volunteers to collect the information or data. Write the names and due dates next to each action on your team log.
3. Follow up with those volunteers to look at the data they have collected. With those volunteers, make a decision whether this idea is now Level 1 or Level 2.
4. Give recognition to the volunteers who collected the data.
5. Follow the previous steps for Level 1 or Level 2 ideas.

Appendix VII: FORMS

On the following pages are copies of all the forms to make this process clear and easy. Feel free to copy them for use within your organization.

Roadmap on Your Journey to Results through Engagement

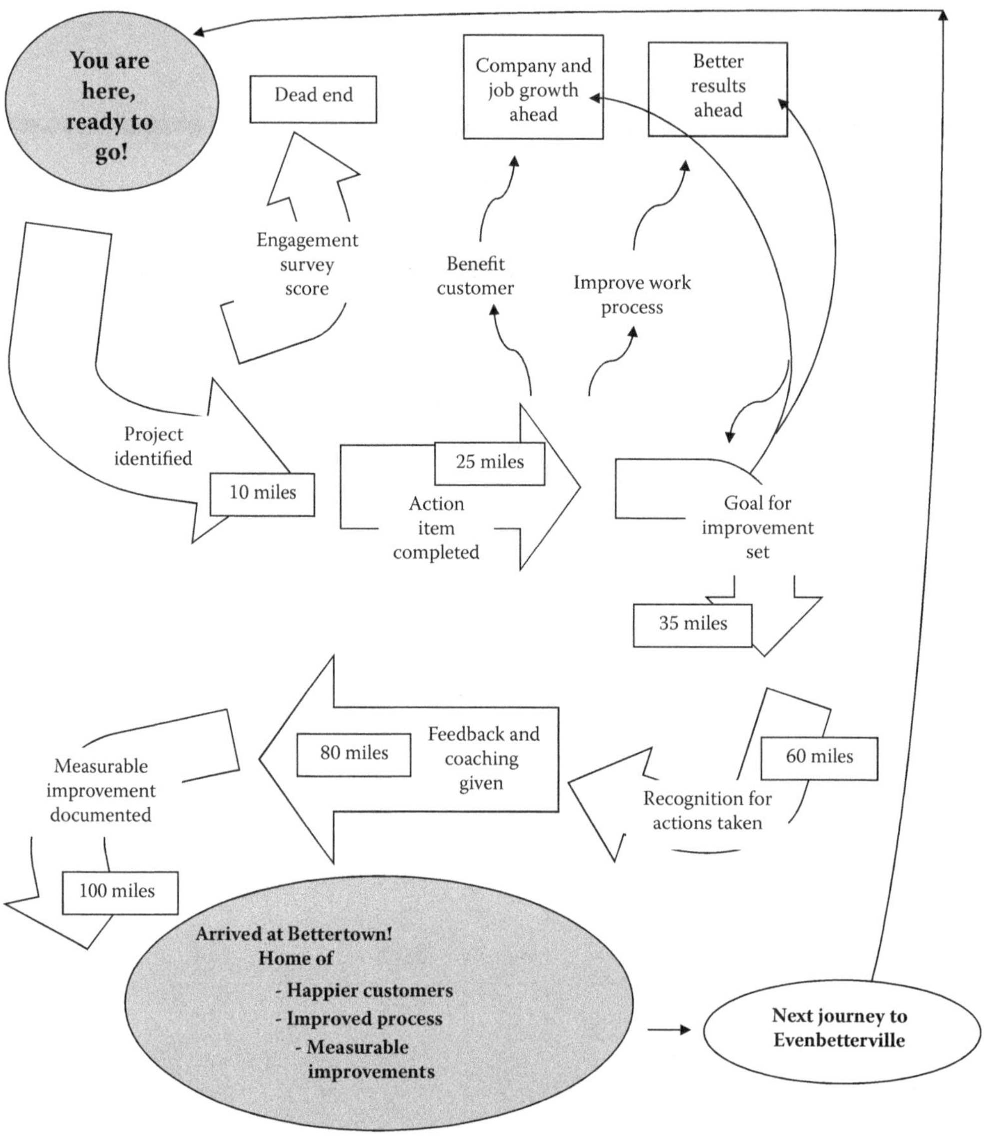

Quick quiz: How far along are you?

Mark the Miles on Your Engagement Journey: Actions Completed (document your actions and circle your miles earned)				
		Date Completed	By Whom	Miles Earned
1.	Project identified			10
2.	One person has completed one action item to get the project started (repeat to involve more people)			15
3.	Goal for improvement is set			15
4.	Feedback and coaching given			20
5.	Positive recognition given to individual(s)			20
6.	Improvement measured and documented			20
			Total miles	

Team Log for __________________ (team)				
Date: ________________ Project: ____________________________________				
Idea	Action Step	Volunteer	Target Date	Status

Sample Project: Checklist for Ideas to Implementation	
1. Name the problem or project.	"Our customers want delivery 100% to schedule. We're now at 76%."
2. Ask for ideas to solve or improve. Write down all ideas.	"How can we reduce our cycle time to reach this goal?"
3. Select one to three ideas to test by voting.	"We've brainstormed 11 ideas. Vote for the three that you think are most likely to help, based on your knowledge and experience."
4. Level those ideas.	"Let's take these three ideas through the leveling template to determine the actions we can take now. Please volunteer for the action items you can take during the next week."
5. Log, implement, and test the ideas.	"Please write your action item (including testing an idea), your name, and due date on our team log.
6. Measure effectiveness and make action plan.	"We'll review the log in one week and ask for any data you've observed with your test. Based on that data, we'll decide whether to implement the idea."

Coaching Checklist	
1.	Ask the employee what she needs to learn, or the tools or materials she needs, in order to complete the action steps. Ask her if she already knows parts of it.
2.	Together, create a step-by-step plan for her behaviors to perform these substeps. Create a checklist showing these steps with target dates.
3.	Train her or arrange for training if needed. Her training must include her actually *practicing* the skill, not just watching someone else do them.
4.	Ask her to mark her progress on the checklist and take the initiative to review it with you daily or every few days (ask her to come and show you her checklist without waiting for you to ask). Ask her to set a schedule for this review and put the dates and times on both your calendars.
5.	Give her specific recognition (positive comments, notes, or both) for each step she completes.

Coaching Plan for (name) ________________ **Coach** ________________

Skill Needed

______________________________ ____________

1 Write in your steps to perform below, with dates. Fill in the box (make a bar graph) when achieved.

Steps to Complete the Project							
Step 6: ______							
Step 5: ______							
Step 4: ______							
Step 3: ______							
Step 2: ______							
Step 1: ______							
Dates: ______ ______ ______ ______ ______ ______							

	______
2	Steps I can already do:
3	Steps where I'll need additional skills:
4	Training plan with dates:
5	Dates I'll review my progress with my coach:
6	Coach: Comments about progress

Template for Giving Positive Recognition

Start by calling your coworker's name: ______________________

Name her *specific* behavior that you value: ______________________

____

State how it helps your department or organization: ______________

____

bravo

To: ______________________________

I like what you did . . .

From: ______________________________

Project Graph Measuring: ________________(results) **Department: ________________________**							
100%							**Goal** -----
95%							
90%							
85%							
80%							
75%							
WeekEnding	Baseline	/ Date	/ Date	/ Date	/ Date	/ Date	/ Date

Leader's Checklist for Recognizing Engagement Actions by Employees							
Leader's name:________________________________ □ Jot the initials of the person who did the activity or activities below □ Tell the person(s) you noticed!							
1.	Took initiative to help a coworker						
2.	Offered ideas for solutions and improvements						
3.	Acknowledged others' accomplishments						
4.	Quickly volunteered to lead or assist in projects outside immediate job						
5.	Other:						

Overall Checklist for Leader Standard Work to Engage, Involve, and Motivate Employees through Projects Leader's Name: ______________________							
Leader/Supervisor Actions		Initials of Person(s) with Whom I Took These Actions					
		M	T	W	T	F	S
1.	Asked for ideas for specific improvements						
2.	Formed project team (if needed)						
3.	Coached, set goals, gave feedback						
4.	Gave positive recognition for productive behaviors I saw (and positive solutions I heard)						
5.	Trained tasks, delegated to develop skills						
6.	Called individual by name						

Lessons Learned from Our Projects		
What We Did	What Went Wrong	What We Learned

Lessons Learned from Successes in Our Projects		
What We Did	What Went Well	What We Learned

Glossary

baseline: measurement of past performance before your team makes changes. Baseline gives you something to compare your progress to, so you'll know if your changes are making a difference.

behavior: an action you see someone doing.

brainstorming: a quick way to generate a large number of ideas. The brainstorming leader asks for ideas on a specific topic and records *all* ideas with no judgment.

celebration: a gathering after an accomplishment to review our behaviors that made our success happen. We reminisce and tell stories about what we did to succeed—a "party" form of Proud Time.

coach: help someone learn a behavior that will help will help him or her become more successful; help develop a skill.

communication: words, actions, body language, facial expressions, documents, and signs that send messages to other people.

coworkers: everyone we work with in our organizations (up, down, and sideways).

culture: the actions and words in an organization for which people show approval or disapproval; often informal and not written down—"the way we do things around here."

discretionary effort: the time, work, and ideas that an employee gives *above* what it takes to "just get by" (or the minimum requirements of the job).

80/20 rule: a rule of thumb stating that 80% of outcomes can be attributed to 20% of the causes for a given event (also known as the *Pareto Principle*).

engage: to gain and hold attention and interest; to ask to participate

feedback: information on performance that helps an individual know how to improve.

goal: the measurable result we want to achieve.

graph: data posted visually showing baseline, goal, and actual performance. Dots, lines, or bars show a trend over a time period.

Hippocratic oath: "First, do no harm," from the physician's vow dating back to the father of medicine, Hippocrates.

involve: to help people take actions.

leader standard work: checklist of actions supervisors are expected to take daily, weekly, or monthly.

lean leadership: taking initiative to improve work processes.

leveling: the process to determine whether ideas can be implemented or tested right away (Level 1), need approvals (Level 2), or need more information (Level 3).

listen: understand another person's message before offering a response (could you pass a quiz on what the person said?).

motivate: to inspire a person to *want* to do something.

***muda*:** waste (from Japanese); wasted material, effort, time, money.

***muri*:** strain (from Japanese) due to the positions or motions required to do the job, or too much work for one person.

positive recognition: acknowledging a person for his or her actions, causing him or her to want to repeat those actions.

proud time: to make time to recognize an individual's or team's accomplishments; can be initiated by either the person who wishes to share her or his accomplishment or by a leader or coworker.

pull method: in Lean process, wait for a customer order (internal or external) before producing a product or service.

push method: to create a product for "stock" (hoping a customer will order it later).

recognition: see *positive recognition.*

seven traditional wastes of Lean: what we aim to reduce or eliminate—waste in transport, inventory, motion, waiting, overprocessing, overproduction, and defects.

subgoals: small, incremental improvements leading to a final goal.

team: also "group." Ideally four to six people who meet once or several times to improve processes and results. Members may work in the same department or may represent several departments (determined by the issue(s) the team will address).

time goal: the target date to complete an action step.

trust: the experience that someone tells the truth. She will do what she says she will do; her actions match her words.

two-way commitment: both leader and employee do what they say they will do; both let each other be the first to know of any problems with the other.

Resources

Books

Sustain Your Gains: The People Side of Lean-Six Sigma, by Michael McCarthy (Performance Management Publications, 2011). Accelerate improvement and sustain your gains from Lean and Six Sigma. This book combines Lean process and systematic behavioral methods. Stop losing your hard-won Lean and Six Sigma gains. www.the5sstore.com

You Made My Day: Creating Co-Worker Recognition & Relationships, by Janis Allen and Michael McCarthy (Performance Leadership Publications, 2005). Build teamwork and performance by showing employees, supervisors, and managers how to give positive recognition. Build a more positive culture from the bottom up. www.janisallen.com

Bringing Out the Best in People, by Aubrey C. Daniels (Performance Management Publications, 2000). How to use behavior-based performance management ideas to transform employees' work into something they're willing, ready, and even eager to do. www.aubreydaniels.com

Performance Management: Changing Behavior That Drives Organizational Effectiveness, 5th edition), by Aubrey C. Daniels and Jon S. Bailey (Performance Management Publications, 2004). Based on evidence and research that shows how to transform or create a positive culture and a safety culture. Topics include what leaders need to do more of, how to spark innovation, and how to manage multigenerational workforces. www.aubrey-daniels.com

5S Made Easy: A Step-by-Step Guide to Implementing and Sustaining Your 5S Program, by David Visco (CRC Press, 2015). In-depth guidance on how to implement and sustain each of the 5S pillars—sort, set in order, shine, standardize, and sustain. Includes "before" and "after" pictures of real-world 5S solutions and useful forms. www.the5sstore.com

Video

Communication Can Make or Break Your Day (27-minute video DVD) by Janis Allen and Michael McCarthy (Performance Leadership Publications, 2014). Improve your communication skills—supervisor to employee, employee to supervisor, and peer-to-peer. Tools to reduce the negative talk around you and increase the positive talk, problem solve without finger-pointing, and use positive motivation to improve engagement and create a more positive culture. www.janisallen.com

Audio

Do's & Don'ts for Delivering Recognition (and Receiving It) for Teams, Co-Workers, and Supervisors (1-hour CD), by Janis Allen, interviewed by Michael McCarthy (Performance Leadership Publications, 2013). Practical tips for giving positive recognition that doesn't cost a dime. How to overcome skepticism of your receivers. How to prevent blunders and deal effectively with recognition resistors. www.janisallen.com

Webinars (Customized for your organization)

Sustain Your Gains: Training for quality managers, CI professionals, supervisors, and managers to sustain your gains from Lean-Six Sigma using PBM (Process Behavior Maintenance). Three one-hour sessions spaced one to two weeks apart, with on-the-job practice and assignments, for up to 12 participants. Delivered via the internet, on-site training available.

Contact: mikemccarthy@sustainleangains.com

Engage, Involve, and Motivate Your Employees: Training for training directors, supervisors, managers, and HR professionals to implement the tools in this book. Additional techniques for giving positive recognition. Three 45-minute sessions delivered live to your supervisors or team leaders, either in person or via the Internet. Spaced one week apart with action assignments in between. Don't just get trained, get started! To learn how to make this work for you, contact mikemccarthy@sustainleangains.com

Supplies

5S

Everything you need to implement 5S. Along with 5S expertise they have red tags, tool shadow boards, posters, signs, custom visual solutions, heavy-duty floor tape, and more. www.the5Sstore.com

Recognition

Cards and tips to give meaningful recognition and appreciation.
http://recognitionworks.net/toolkits/

Culture

Winning Ways to a Positive Culture, deck of 52 playing cards to make learning and doing fun. Grouped in four "suites" or categories: Recognition, Teamwork, Positive Culture, and Customer Service, 52 specific ideas you and your employees can implement in your workplace immediately for culture change you can see and hear. Contact: janisallen@janisallen.com

Websites

www.sustainleangains.com
www.janisallen.com
www.recognitionworks.net
www.the5Sstore.com

EIM Trainer Certification

Are you a plant manager, training manager, continuous improvement coordinator, safety supervisor, or human resources manager? If so, you may want to be certified to conduct EIM (Engagement, Involvement, and Motivation) training.

Contact: mikemccarthy@sustainleangains.com

Index

Akers, Paul, 28

Baseline, 74
Berra, Yogi, 25
Brainstorming, 36, 139
Bringing Out the Best in People (Daniels), 104

Celebrations, 60, 70–72
Coach/coaching, 47–50
  and correct behaviors, 109–116
  projects, 48–50
Communication skills, 48, 74, 93
Correct behaviors, and engagement, 109–116
Culture, 60, 93

Daniels, Aubrey C., vii, 104
Decision-making skills, 48
Discretionary effort, 60–61

Engagement
  and correct behaviors, 109–116
  description, 2–7
  five steps of, 17–19
  forms, 146–154
  frequently made mistakes (FMMs), 117–124
  harming motivation, 7–8
  and idea levels, 141–143
  involving people, 14
  launch guide to, 129–130
  measurable goals, 11–13
  overview, 1–2
  and pinch points, 131–132
  and Project PULL, 81–88, 125–126
  WD-40 tips, 133–134

FastCap LLC, 28
Feedback, 74, 76
FIND and FIX problems, 28–29
FMMs, *see* Frequently made mistakes (FMMs)
Frequently made mistakes (FMMs), 117–124

Gemba walks, 106, 107
General skills, 82
Georgion, Mike, 125, 126
Graphs, 74–76

Helping People Win at Work (Ridge), 122

Ideas
  levels and engagement, 141–143
  for project improvements, 35–46
    acknowledgement, 41–42
    asking help, 36–41
    levels, 43–46
    team involvement, 41
    testing, 42–43
Individual initiative, 28

Johnson & Johnson, 122
Juran, Joseph M., vii

Kaizen process improvement events, 28

Leaders/leadership skills, 48, 125–128
  and trust, 93–102
Leader Standard Work checklist, 107–108
Leveling, 36

McCarthy, Michael, vii
Measurable project data, 126
Milliken & Company, 125
Motivation
  and positive recognition, 59–72
  and projects, 89–92

Positive recognition
  celebrations, 60, 70–72
  discretionary effort, 60–61
  effective ways, 63–69
  ideas and actions, 61–63
  and motivation, 59–72
  proud time, 60, 69–70
Problem-solving skills, 48
Project PULL, 21–34, 81–88, 125–126
  and PUSH, 31–34
Projects
  and coach/coaching, 47–50
  coaching, 48–50
  completion of, 79
  ideas for improvements, 35–46
    acknowledgement, 41–42
    asking help, 36–41
    levels, 43–46
    team involvement, 41
    testing, 42–43
  measurable improvement, 103–108
  and motivation, 89–92
  recognition, 50–55
  and recognition, 47, 50–56
  and team selection, 135–138
  and time goal/time target, 47–48
Proud time, 60, 69–70

"Quality First" program, 96–97

Recognition, 47
  positive (*see* Positive recognition)
  projects, 50–56
Ridge, Garry, 73, 122
Robertson, Michel J., vii
Rogers, Orelia, 99
Rother, Mike, 50

Socrates, 49
Socratic method, 49, 126

Taiichi Ohno, 23
Team selection, and project, 135–138
Technical skills, 48
Time goal/time targets, 47–48
Toolbox Meetings, 107
The Toyota Coaching Kata, 49–50
Trust, and leadership skills, 93–102
2 Second Lean (video), 28
Tylenol, 122

WD-40 Company, 126, 133–134